Sara
Compl

D0446621

Blasted, Phaedra's L
4.48 Psychosis, Skin

'Kane was a dramatist original enough to communicate ultimate emotions with a strange beauty as well as with a frightening bluntness.' *The Times*

Blasted: 'Kane has an acute grasp of sexual politics and her dialogue is both sparse and stunning. They will call her mad, but then they said that about Strindberg.' *Mail on Sunday*

Phaedra's Love: '*Phaedra's Love* is pure drama, and it doesn't attempt naturalism, however pertinent its ideas. Kane never seeks to manipulate us emotionally, and so earns our respect.' *What's On*

Cleansed: 'For better or worse, the spell of most plays drifts off the moment you leave the theatre. Not Sarah Kane's *Cleansed*. Hard as you try, its compelling, horror-soaked atmosphere refuses to be shaken off. It clings to you like a shroud.' *Independent*

Crave: 'A dramatic poem in the late-Beckett style, sometimes a chamber quartet for lost voices.' *The Times*

4.48 Psychosis: 'The beauty and rawness . . . – the combination of unprocessed honesty and meticulous craft – remains as striking as ever; Kane's power to take material beyond endurance and shape it, burnish it, laugh at it, dominate with her art.' *Scotsman*

Sarah Kane was born in 1971. Her first play, *Blasted*, was produced at the Royal Court Theatre Upstairs in 1995. Her second play, *Phaedra's Love*, was produced at the Gate Theatre in 1996. In April 1998, *Cleansed* was produced at the Royal Court Theatre Downstairs, and in September 1998, *Crave* was produced by Paines Plough and Bright Ltd at the Traverse Theatre, Edinburgh. Her last play, *4.48 Psychosis*, premiered at the Royal Court Jerwood Theatre Upstairs in June 2000. Her short film, *Skin*, produced by British Screen/Channel Four, premiered in June 1997. Sarah Kane died in 1999.

SARAH KANE

Complete Plays

Blasted
Phaedra's Love
Cleansed
Crave
4.48 Psychosis
Skin

introduced by David Greig

Methuen Drama

METHUEN DRAMA CONTEMPORARY DRAMATISTS

15 17 19 20 18 16 14

This collection first published in 2001 by Methuen Publishing Ltd

Methuen Drama
A & C Black Publishers Ltd
38 Soho Square
London W1D 3HB
www.acblack.com

Blasted first published in 1995 by Methuen in *Frontline Intelligence 2*
copyright © 1995 Sarah Kane, 2006 Estate of Sarah Kane
Phaedra's Love first published in 1996 by Methuen
copyright © 1996 Sarah Kane, 2006 Estate of Sarah Kane
Cleansed first published in 1998 by Methuen
copyright © 1998 Sarah Kane, 2006 Estate of Sarah Kane
Crave first published in 1998 by Methuen
copyright © 1998 Sarah Kane, 2006 Estate of Sarah Kane
4.48 Psychosis first published in 2000 by Methuen
copyright © 2000 Sarah Kane, 2006 Estate of Sarah Kane
Skin copyright © 1997 Sarah Kane, 2006 Estate of Sarah Kane

Introduction copyright © David Greig 2001

Sarah Kane has asserted her rights in accordance with the Copyright, Designs
and Patents Act, 1988, to be identified as the author of this work

A CIP catalogue record for this book
is available from the British Library

ISBN 978-0413-742605

Typeset by Deltatype Ltd, Birkenhead
Printed and bound in Great Britain by
Cox & Wyman Ltd, Reading, Berkshire

Caution

Contents

Chronology

January 1995	*Blasted*, Royal Court Theatre Upstairs
May 1996	*Phaedra's Love*, Gate Theatre
June 1997	*Skin*, Channel 4
April 1998	*Cleansed*, Royal Court Theatre Downstairs
August 1998	*Crave*, Traverse Theatre
June 2000	*4.48 Psychosis*, Royal Court Jerwood Theatre Upstairs

Introduction

Sarah Kane is best known for the way her career began, in the extraordinary public controversy over *Blasted*, and the way it ended: in her suicide and the posthumous production of her last play, *4.48 Psychosis*. Both were shocking and defining moments in recent British theatre and their shadows are bound to haunt any reading of her work. But it would be a pity if these extraordinary events were to distract from the qualities of the five plays she left behind; a pity if, in attending to the mythology of the author, we were to miss the explosive theatricality, the lyricism, the emotional power, and the bleak humour that is contained within the plays themselves.

Blasted, Phaedra's Love, Cleansed, Crave and *4.48 Psychosis* add up to a body of work which pushed recklessly at the naturalistic boundaries of British theatre. Each play was a new step on an artistic journey in which Kane mapped the darkest and most unforgiving internal landscapes: landscapes of violation, of loneliness, of power, of mental collapse and, most consistently, the landscape of love.

Blasted was produced by the Royal Court in January 1995 in the sixty-seat Theatre Upstairs. The play begins with a middle-aged man, Ian, and a young woman, Cate, entering an expensive hotel room in Leeds. The stage immediately suggests the kind of chamber piece about relationships with which the British theatre-goer is so familiar. And yet, almost from the play's first words, 'I've shat in better places than this', there is an uneasy awareness that this play is not behaving itself. Ian's behaviour and language are unpleasant, repulsive even, and yet nothing in the writing is condemning him. No authorial voice is leading us to safety. As the play progresses, the moral unease grows until the scene finally changes and we learn that, during the night, Ian has raped Cate. Shortly afterwards, there is a knock on the hotel room door and, in the play's most daring moment, a soldier enters, apparently from nowhere, and brings in with him the terrifying fragments of a world blown apart by violence.

It is as though the act of rape, which blasts the inner world of both victim and perpetrator, has also destroyed the world outside the room. The play's form begins to fragment. Its structure seems to buckle under the weight of the violent forces it has unleashed. The time frame condenses; a scene that begins in spring ends in summer. The dialogue erodes, becoming sparse. The scenes are presented in smaller and smaller fragments until they are a series of snapshots: images of Ian, all the structures of his life destroyed, reduced to his base essence – a human being, weeping, shitting, lonely, broken, dying and, in the play's final moments, comforted.

The final images are not unlike those moments in Beckett where the human impulse to connect is found surviving in the most bleak and crushing places. Those critics who drew attention to *Blasted*'s litany of broken taboos missed the fact that the play's roots were not in the bloodbaths of postmodern cinema but in the Shakespearean anatomies of reduced men: Lear on the heath and Timon in his cave.

Blasted placed Kane on the news pages of tabloids as well as the arts pages of broadsheets. While other playwrights might have relished the sort of impact her play created, for Kane it was difficult and depressing. Her simple premise, that there was a connection between a rape in a Leeds hotel room and the hellish devastation of civil war, had been critically misunderstood as a childish attempt to shock. It would not be until *Crave* in 1998 that public perceptions of her work would begin to move beyond the simplistic responses of the *Blasted* controversy.

Kane's next play was a rewriting of the Phaedra myth commissioned by the tiny and underfunded Gate Theatre in Notting Hill. The project, and the Gate itself, which specialises in producing European works in translation, provided a natural refuge for her writing to develop. *Phaedra's Love*, which she also directed, saw her continue the process of fragmenting naturalism. Again, the world of the stage is dark and extreme but now the source of pain has narrowed down from civil war to war within the family. In this instance, a royal family. It is also the first of Kane's plays to deal explicitly with what was to become her main theme: love.

Hippolytus, the spoiled prince, is driven to preserve his self inviolate. Emotions, love in particular, and need of any type are an unbearable threat to him. His uncontrollable sexual impulse, which would otherwise draw him into contact with others, must express itself in masturbation or in the degradation of his sexual partners into objects. Phaedra, his stepmother, is in love with her son. Her drive to submit herself to the impossibility of her desire, to lose herself within it, is the opposite of Hippolytus's and forms the second of the twin impulses that move the family towards a violent destruction.

The sheer impossibility of survival in either of these emotional conditions, total self-abnegation or total self-preservation, forms the bleak backdrop to Phaedra's journey. Abused by Hippolytus, she finds the ultimate self-destruction in suicide. Hippolytus, publicly accused of his mother's rape, refuses to defend himself and is torn apart by the mob. He remains, in his mordant final line, emotionally intact, even as his body is dismembered and its fragments lie about him.

In Phaedra and Hippolytus, Kane marked out the two poles that are the extremes of the human response to love. She also exposed the bitter irony, which is that those of one pole are driven to seek out those of the other. Brittle and full of bleak insight, *Phaedra's Love* contains some of Kane's wittiest dialogue. Perhaps the humour comes from its authorial detachment. Poised, bored, and often cynical, it is almost as though the play's whole voice belongs to Hippolytus. In her next play, *Cleansed*, Kane seemed to switch poles and allow the voices of self-abnegation to carry the weight of the play.

Cleansed took yet another step away from Naturalism. Learning from Büchner (whose masterpiece *Woyzeck* she directed in 1997), Kane stripped away the mechanics of explanatory narrative and presented the audience with a series of poetic images and pared dialogue. The play concerns the inhabitants of an institution under the control of a torturer/psychiatrist named Tinker. Each inmate is in love with another, but Tinker sadistically tests each love to find its limits. The play focuses on a central question: what is the most that one lover can truthfully promise another? An insane experimenter, Tinker drives the characters to the extremes of pain in order to find out what power love has over them.

Under the relentless pressure of Tinker's sadism the characters' bodies begin to break apart. Limbs are removed, skins removed, genitals removed, and identities forcibly changed until, in the play's final scenes, each inhabitant carries the fragments of someone else's identity. The Woman says she is Grace, Grace looks like Graham, Carl wears Robin's clothes. Unable to love and unable to cease loving, the characters find refuge in mutability, transcending their own limits. These gender confusions, the play's lyricism and its central theme of a sister searching for a lost brother reflect another Shakespearean influence on Kane: *Twelfth Night*.

Cleansed was regarded as the bleakest and most difficult of Kane's plays to date and it is certainly a punishing theatrical experience. Yet, reading it again, it seems surprisingly redemptive. As she did with Ian in *Blasted* and Hippolytus in *Phaedra's Love*, Kane finds in Tinker, whose actions are psychotically wicked, the same humanity that she finds in the characters who suffer his torments. She also finds in Rod's promise, 'I love you now. I'm with you now. I'll do my best, moment to moment, not to betray you. Now. That's it. No more. Don't make me lie to you,' a foundation for love which, although austere, is none the less strong enough to survive the most appalling tests.

Theatrically, *Cleansed* is a daring challenge. Its physicalisation of lyrical imagery raises the same question that dogs Kane's first three plays: how do-able are they? With its stage directions like 'the rats carry Carl's feet away', or 'a sunflower bursts through the floor', it would be natural for the reader to question the practicality of staging

the work. This is a question that goes to the heart of
Kane's writing. Every one of her plays asks the director to
make radical staging decisions, whether it is how to
represent violence in *Blasted*, how to represent rats in
Cleansed or what visual context to give the voices in *Crave*.
In a Kane play the author makes demands but she does
not provide solutions.

Kane believed passionately that if it was possible to
imagine something, it was possible to represent it. By
demanding an interventionist and radical approach from
her directors she was forcing them to go to the limits of
their theatrical imagination, forcing them into poetic and
expressionist solutions. Her stage imagery poses no
problems for theatre per se, only for a theatre tied to
journalistic naturalism. Nothing in a Kane play is any more
bizarre than Shakespeare's direction at the end of *A Winter's
Tale* 'The statue comes to life.' With *Cleansed*, Kane wrote a
play which demanded that its staging be as poetic as its
writing.

Blasted and *Cleansed* had been conceived as the first two
parts of a trilogy of plays, the last of which was to be
concerned with nuclear devastation. Interestingly, Kane
abandoned the idea of a trilogy after *Cleansed* and instead
she pushed her writing in a new and surprising direction.

Since autumn 1996 Kane had worked as Writer in
Residence for Paines Plough, the new writing company
based in London. As part of her role she was involved with
the process of developing new plays and new writers. One
of the company's initiatives was a series of lunchtime play
readings at the Bridewell Theatre. These readings provided
a suitably low-key opportunity for Kane to present a piece
which she had written quickly in response to a gap in the
programme, and which was an experiment in an open
textual form. This new play, *Crave*, was presented initially,
at the reading, under the pseudonym Marie Kelvedon;
partly a private joke and partly a serious attempt to allow
her work to escape, briefly, from the shadow of being
'Sarah Kane, the controversial author of *Blasted*'.

Crave is divided into four voices, identified only by the

letters A, B, M and C. The voices speak without concrete
context and there is only the most fragmentary hint of a
narrative. The voices describe their desires, remember losses
in the past, and question their future in the face of their
psychological damage. Binding the whole piece, as in
Cleansed, is the exploration of love's assault upon the
wholeness of the self. She draws upon many forms of love:
primarily sexual love, maternal love and abusive love.
Unlike in *Cleansed*, however, in *Crave* one can almost feel the
intoxicating release of Kane's writing as the borderlines of
character evaporate entirely and her imagery moves from
physical to textual realisation.

The effect of the piece when staged is surprisingly
musical. The text demands attendance to its rhythms in
performance, revealing its meanings not line by line but,
rather like a string quartet, in the hypnotic play of different
voices and themes. Four voices become one. This effect is
replicated in the stage image. The overwhelming impression
is that the four voices are, in fact, voices from within and
without one individual life, yet the stage is occupied by four
physically real bodies. In the case of the first production,
the bodies were a middle-aged man, a middle-aged woman,
a younger man and a younger woman. The play's form,
and this central, single image – four different bodies
occupying one life – combine to evoke the powerful sense
of a self fragmented.

Crave's elliptical references to specific events clearly
suggest that the author is drawing heavily on personal
experience in the writing. Yet the artistic triumph of the
piece is that this personal quality does not close the play off
to the viewer. One example is the tender love speech which
is given to A. The list of desires is so specific that one feels
it must be it must be true to the writer in some sense. And
yet the overall effect of the specificity is, perversely, to
render it true more generally. It is as though by excavating
herself rather than attempting to capture an invented
character's consciousness, Kane has opened her writing out
to the audience, leaving a space in which they can place
themselves and their own experience. It is a comment on

the complexity and compassion of her writing that this
desperately tender speech is spoken on stage by an older
man whose voice, within the text, is given the memories
and desires of an abuser.

Crave enjoyed great critical success at the Edinburgh
Festival. Perhaps the critics felt that, by changing her style,
Kane had allowed them to engage more easily with her
work. Yet, as well as being a departure, *Crave* also
represents a definite continuation of the formal and
thematic paths she had been following for the previous
three plays.

The liquid, poetic voice of *Crave*, and its obviously
personal resonances, perhaps imply an author who was
creating work by simply tapping into her unconscious and
letting the words flow. But Kane was a playwright who was
acutely aware of her work's context in the history of
theatre. While her voice was powerful and unique it also
owed a great deal to the playwrights whose work she
admired: Büchner, Beckett, Bond and Barker for example.
Under the auspices of both Paines Plough and the Royal
Court's European Summer School, Kane ran writers'
groups and led workshops with emerging playwrights. It
would have been pointless for Kane to lead workshops like
these unless she was thinking critically about the structural
possibilities of the medium. To read her plays, for all their
pain, as raw, is to overlook the complex artfulness of their
construction.

Crave ends in a falling towards light. It is, like *Cleansed*
and *Blasted*, an ambiguous redemption. The ambiguity lying
in that falling which is both a liberating shedding of the self
and also the self-destruction of death.

Kane had been plagued throughout her life by bouts of
depression. With each occurrence, her depression became
more debilitating and, ultimately, she became suicidal.
Towards the end of the summer of 1998 she began to
succumb to another depressive episode. It was her
experience of this, and the treatments she received for it
which formed the material of her next play. A play which
is perhaps uniquely painful for the reader in that it appears

to have been written in the almost certain knowledge that it would be performed posthumously. *4.48 Psychosis* was written throughout the autumn and winter of 1998/99. On 20th February 1999, Kane committed suicide.

For a period of her depression, Kane had found herself awoken, every morning, at 4.48 a.m. She took this moment, the darkest hour, just before dawn, and found in it a moment of great clarity, a moment when the confusions of psychosis seem to evaporate. The paradox in the play is that the moment of clarity in the psychotic mind is, to those outside it, the moment when delusion is at its strongest.

In the text, Kane pushed further still the formal elements she had explored in *Crave*. This time there are no delineated voices, and no textual indication of the number or gender of the performers. The same fragmentation of self, the losing of borders that the psychotic mind experiences, is literally reflected in the structure of the piece. The writing consists of monologues and fragments of dialogues taking place between figures that resemble a doctor and a patient. Unnamed, the voice of authority might also be a lover, a friend, or perhaps the patient's own dialogue with themself. The whole play describes the internal landscape of a suicidal psychosis. A landscape more extreme and pitiless even than those described in the four previous plays.

4.48 Psychosis sees the ultimate narrowing of Kane's focus in her work. The struggle of the self to remain intact has moved from civil war, into the family, into the couple, into the individual and finally into the theatre of psychosis: the mind itself. 'And my mind is the subject of these bewildered fragments,' the play's voice states. Yet perhaps it is as well to be cautious here. Whose mind? The mind of the speaker of the words in the theatre, definitely, but does that directly mean the mind of the author? Kane's work has constantly shown the self to be a problematic and fluid entity, shifting and struggling against its own limits, and transforming. Why should her authorial self be any different? *4.48 Psychosis* is not a letter from one person to

another but a play, intended to be voiced by at least one
and probably more actors. The mind that is the subject of
the play's fragments is the psychotic mind. A mind which is
the author, and which is also more than the author. It's a
mind that the play's open form allows the audience to enter
and recognise themselves within.

The play was finally produced in June 2000 at the Royal
Court Jerwood Theatre Upstairs, directed by Kane's long-
time collaborator, James Macdonald. Macdonald split the
play's voice into three: two women and one man. The
three voices, in part, representing the division of a person
into victim/perpetrator/bystander. A division which
catalyses the play. Reading backwards, which is always
dangerous, one can see that this division is itself a
culmination of the ideas in the four previous plays. *Blasted*'s
Ian, for example, is a journalist bystander who becomes a
perpetrator and, finally, a victim. In Kane's writing the
three figures, always contained within the single body, serve
as an honest and compassionate anatomy of the human
experience of pain.

The voice of the play, led through therapy and endless
medication, neither of which is able to alleviate the
suffering, talks to the doctor with a sardonic wit. The dark
comedy in the description of the drugs prescribed and their
negligible effects remind one of Lear on the heath
demanding the impossible of his apothecary: 'sweeten my
imagination'.

4.48 Psychosis is a report from a region of the mind that
most of us hope never to visit but from which many people
cannot escape. Those trapped there are normally rendered
voiceless by their condition. That the play was written
whilst suffering from depression, which is a destructive
rather than a creative condition, was an act of generosity
by the author. That the play is artistically successful is
positively heroic.

Suicide always poses a question, and the suicide of a
writer leaves material over which the living can only pore
in the search for answers. Inevitably, the shadow of Kane's
death will fall across her plays and one can find oneself

reading them in search of diagnoses, listening out for
unheard cries for help. The challenge for the reader in
Kane's last two plays is not to search for the author behind
the words but to freight the plays with our own presence,
our own fears of the self-destructive act and our own
impulses towards it.

Something like the sound of a door shutting haunts the
word 'complete'. *The Complete Sarah Kane*. In the silence after
completion other voices gather, interpreting, analysing and
decoding the work until, eventually, the plays themselves
can come to seem only palimpsests, barely glimpsed
beneath the commentary. Kane, herself, never supplied an
author's note to her plays, and she distrusted introductions
to the plays of others, believing that if a play was any good
it would speak for itself. With this in mind, whoever
approaches the plays in this volume – reader, actor, or
director – should remain sceptical of interpretations;
sceptical of my interpretation as much as any other. The
texts contained here are, undoubtedly, good plays and as
such they will speak for themselves. To read these plays for
what they tell us about their author is, to my mind, a
pointlessly forensic act. The work's true completion comes
when the plays are read for what they tell us about
ourselves.

                                                    David Greig

Blasted

For Vincent O'Connell, with thanks.

Blasted was first performed at the Royal Court Theatre Upstairs, London, on 12 January 1995. The cast was as follows:

Ian	Pip Donaghy
Cate	Kate Ashfield
Soldier	Dermot Kerrigan

Directed by James Macdonald
Designed by Franziska Wilcken
Lighting by Jon Linstrum
Sound by Paul Arditti

Characters

Ian
Cate
Soldier

Author's note

Punctuation is used to indicate delivery, not to conform to the rules of grammar.

A stroke (/) marks the point of interruption in overlapping dialogue.

Words in square brackets [ ] are not spoken, but have been included in the text to clarify meaning.

Stage directions in brackets ( ) function as lines.

Editor's note

This edition of *Blasted*, first reprinted in 2000, incorporates minor revisions made to the original text by Sarah Kane shortly before her death. It should therefore be regarded as the definitive version in all respects.

Scene One

A very expensive hotel room in Leeds – the kind that is so expensive it could be anywhere in the world.

There is a large double bed.
A mini-bar and champagne on ice.
A telephone.
A large bouquet of flowers.
Two doors – one is the entrance from the corridor, the other leads off to the bathroom.

Two people enter – **Ian** *and* **Cate**.

Ian *is 45, Welsh born but lived in Leeds much of his life and picked up the accent.*

Cate *is 21, a lower-middle-class Southerner with a south London accent and a stutter when under stress.*

They enter.

Cate *stops at the door, amazed at the classiness of the room.*
Ian *comes in, throws a small pile of newspapers on the bed, goes straight to the mini-bar and pours himself a large gin.*
He looks briefly out of the window at the street, then turns back to the room.

Ian I've shat in better places than this.

(*He gulps down the gin.*)

I stink.
You want a bath?

Cate (*Shakes her head.*)

Ian *goes into the bathroom and we hear him run the water. He comes back in with only a towel around his waist and a revolver in his hand. He checks it is loaded and puts it under his pillow.*

Ian Tip that wog when he brings up the sandwiches.

He leaves fifty pence and goes into the bathroom.
Cate *comes further into the room.*
She puts her bag down and bounces on the bed.
She goes around the room, looking in every drawer, touching everything.
She smells the flowers and smiles.

Cate   Lovely.

Ian comes back in, hair wet, towel around his waist, drying himself off.
He stops and looks at **Cate** *who is sucking her thumb.*
He goes back in the bathroom where he dresses.
We hear him coughing terribly in the bathroom.
He spits in the sink and re-enters.

Cate   You all right?

Ian   It's nothing.

He pours himself another gin, this time with ice and tonic, and sips it at a more normal pace.
He collects his gun and puts it in his under-arm holster.
He smiles at **Cate**.

Ian   I'm glad you've come. Didn't think you would.

   (*He offers her champagne.*)

Cate   (*Shakes her head.*)

   I was worried.

Ian   This? (*He indicates his chest.*) Don't matter.

Cate   I didn't mean that. You sounded unhappy.

Ian   (*Pops the champagne. He pours them both a glass.*)

Cate   What we celebrating?

Ian   (*Doesn't answer. He goes to the window and looks out.*)
   Hate this city. Stinks. Wogs and Pakis taking over.

Cate   You shouldn't call them that.

Ian Why not?

Cate It's not very nice.

Ian You a nigger-lover?

Cate Ian, don't.

Ian You like our coloured brethren?

Cate Don't mind them.

Ian Grow up.

Cate There's Indians at the day centre where my brother goes. They're really polite.

Ian So they should be.

Cate He's friends with some of them.

Ian Retard, isn't he?

Cate No, he's got learning difficulties.

Ian Aye. Spaz.

Cate No he's not.

Ian Glad my son's not a Joey.

Cate Don't c- call him that.

Ian Your mother I feel sorry for. Two of you like it.

Cate Like wh- what?

Ian (*Looks at her, deciding whether or not to continue. He decides against it.*)

You know I love you.

Cate (*Smiles a big smile, friendly and non-sexual.*)

Ian Don't want you ever to leave.

Cate I'm here for the night.

Ian   (*Drinks.*)

Sweating again. Stink. You ever thought of getting married?

Cate   Who'd marry me?

Ian   I would.

Cate   I couldn't.

Ian   You don't love me. I don't blame you, I wouldn't.

Cate   I couldn't leave Mum.

Ian   Have to one day.

Cate   Why?

Ian   (*Opens his mouth to answer but can't think of one.*)

There is a knock at the door.
Ian *starts, and* **Cate** *goes to answer it.*

Ian   Don't.

Cate   Why not?

Ian   I said.

He takes his gun from the holster and goes to the door.
He listens.
Nothing.

Cate   (*Giggles.*)

Ian   Shh.

He listens.
Still nothing.

Ian   Probably the wog with the sarnies. Open it.

Cate *opens the door.*
There's no one there, just a tray of sandwiches on the floor.
She brings them in and examines them.

Cate   Ham. Don't believe it.

Ian   (*Takes a sandwich and eats it.*)

Champagne?

Cate   (*Shakes her head.*)

Ian   Got something against ham?

Cate   Dead meat. Blood. Can't eat an animal.

Ian   No one would know.

Cate   No, I can't, I actually can't, I'd puke all over the place.

Ian   It's only a pig.

Cate   I'm hungry.

Ian   Have one of these.

Cate   I CAN'T.

Ian   I'll take you out for an Indian.
Jesus, what's this? Cheese.

Cate *beams.*
She separates the cheese sandwiches from the ham ones, and eats.
Ian *watches her.*

Ian   Don't like your clothes.

Cate   (*Looks down at her clothes.*)

Ian   You look like a lesbos.

Cate   What's that?

Ian   Don't look very sexy, that's all.

Cate   Oh.

(*She continues to eat.*)

Don't like your clothes either.

Ian   (*Looks down at his clothes.*
Then gets up, takes them all off and stands in front of her, naked.)

Put your mouth on me.

Cate (*Stares. Then bursts out laughing.*)

Ian No?
Fine.
Because I stink?

Cate (*Laughs even more.*)

> **Ian** *attempts to dress, but fumbles with embarrassment.*
> *He gathers his clothes and goes into the bathroom where he dresses.*
> **Cate** *eats, and giggles over the sandwiches.*
> **Ian** *returns, fully dressed.*
> *He picks up his gun, unloads and reloads it.*

Ian You got a job yet?

Cate No.

Ian Still screwing the taxpayer.

Cate Mum gives me money.

Ian When are you going to stand on your own feet?

Cate I've applied for a job at an advertising agency.

Ian (*Laughs genuinely.*)

No chance.

Cate Why not?

Ian (*Stops laughing and looks at her.*)

Cate. You're stupid. You're never going to get a job.

Cate I am. I am not.

Ian See.

Cate St- Stop it. You're doing it deliberately.

Ian Doing what?

Cate C- Confusing me.

Ian No, I'm talking, you're just too thick to understand.

Cate   I am not, I am not.

> **Cate** *begins to tremble.* **Ian** *is laughing.*
> **Cate** *faints.*
> **Ian** *stops laughing and stares at her motionless body.*

Ian   Cate?

> (*He turns her over and lifts up her eyelids.*
> *He doesn't know what to do.*
> *He gets a glass of gin and dabs some on her face.*)

Cate   (*Sits bolt upright, eyes open but still unconscious.*)

Ian   Fucking Jesus.

Cate   (*Bursts out laughing, unnaturally, hysterically, uncontrollably.*)

Ian   Stop fucking about.

Cate   (*Collapses again and lies still.*)

> **Ian** *stands by helplessly.*
> *After a few moments,* **Cate** *comes round as if waking up in the*
> *morning.*

Ian   What the Christ was that?

Cate   Have to tell her.

Ian   Cate?

Cate   She's in danger.

> (*She closes her eyes and slowly comes back to normal.*
> *She looks at* **Ian** *and smiles.*)

Ian   What now?

Cate   Did I faint?

Ian   That was real?

Cate   Happens all the time.

Ian   What, fits?

Cate   Since Dad came back.

Ian   Does it hurt?

Cate   I'll grow out of it the doctor says.

Ian   How do you feel?

Cate   (*Smiles.*)

Ian   Thought you were dead.

Cate   [I] Suppose that's what it's like.

Ian   Don't do it again, fucking scared me.

Cate   Don't know much about it, I just go. Feels like I'm away for minutes or months sometimes, then I come back just where I was.

Ian   It's terrible.

Cate   I didn't go far.

Ian   What if you didn't come round?

Cate   Wouldn't know. I'd stay there.

Ian   Can't stand it.

(*He goes to the mini-bar and pours himself another large gin and lights a cigarette.*)

Cate   What?

Ian   Death. Not being.

Cate   You fall asleep and then you wake up.

Ian   How do you know?

Cate   Why don't you give up smoking?

Ian   (*Laughs.*)

Cate   You should. They'll make you ill.

Ian   Too late for that.

Cate Whenever I think of you it's with a cigarette and a gin.

Ian Good.

Cate They make your clothes smell.

Ian Don't forget my breath.

Cate Imagine what your lungs must look like.

Ian Don't need to imagine. I've seen.

Cate When?

Ian Last year. When I came round, surgeon brought in this lump of rotting pork, stank. My lung.

Cate He took it out?

Ian Other one's the same now.

Cate But you'll die.

Ian Aye.

Cate Please stop smoking.

Ian Won't make any difference.

Cate Can't they do something?

Ian No. It's not like your brother, look after him he'll be all right.

Cate They die young.

Ian I'm fucked.

Cate Can't you get a transplant?

Ian Don't be stupid. They give them to people with a life. Kids.

Cate People die in accidents all the time, they must have some spare.

Ian Why? What for? Keep me alive to die of cirrhosis in three months' time.

Cate   You're making it worse, speeding it up.

Ian   Enjoy myself while I'm here.

(*He inhales deeply on his cigarette and swallows the last of the gin neat.*)

[I'll] Call that coon, get some more sent up.

Cate   (*Shakes.*)

Ian   Wonder if the conker understands English.

He notices **Cate**'s *distress and cuddles her.*
He kisses her.
She pulls away and wipes her mouth.

Cate   Don't put your tongue in, I don't like it.

Ian   Sorry.

The telephone rings loudly. **Ian** *starts, then answers it.*

Ian   Hello?

Cate   Who is it?

Ian   (*Covers the mouthpiece.*) Shh.

(*Into the mouthpiece.*) Got it here.

(*He takes a notebook from the pile of newspapers and dictates down the phone.*)

A serial killer slaughtered British tourist Samantha Scrace, S – C – R – A – C – E, in a sick murder ritual comma, police revealed yesterday point new par. The bubbly nineteen year old from Leeds was among seven victims found buried in identical triangular tombs in an isolated New Zealand forest point new par. Each had been stabbed more than twenty times and placed face down comma, hands bound behind their backs point new par. Caps up, ashes at the site showed the maniac had stayed to cook a meal, caps down point new par. Samantha comma, a beautiful redhead with dreams of becoming a model comma, was on the trip of a lifetime after finishing her A levels last year point. Samantha's heartbroken mum said yesterday colon quoting, we pray the police will come up with something dash, anything comma, soon point still quoting. The sooner this lunatic is brought to justice the better point end quote new par. The Foreign Office warned tourists Down Under to take extra care point. A spokesman said colon quoting, common sense is the best rule point end quote, copy ends.

(*He listens. Then he laughs.*)

Exactly.

(*He listens.*)

That one again, I went to see her. Scouse tart, spread her legs. No. Forget it. Tears and lies, not worth the space.

(*He presses a button on the phone to connect him to room service.*)

Tosser.

Cate How do they know you're here?

Ian Told them.

Cate Why?

Ian In case they needed me.

Cate Silly. We came here to be away from them.

Ian Thought you'd like this. Nice hotel.

(*Into the mouthpiece.*)

Bring a bottle of gin up, son.

(*He puts the phone down.*)

Cate We always used to go to yours.

Ian That was years ago. You've grown up.

Cate   (*Smiles.*)

Ian   I'm not well any more.

Cate   (*Stops smiling.*)

> **Ian** *kisses her.*
> *She responds.*
> *He puts his hand under her top and moves it towards her breast.*
> *With the other hand he undoes his trousers and starts masturbating.*
> *He begins to undo her top.*
> *She pushes him away.*

Cate   Ian, d- don't.

Ian   What?

Cate   I don't w- want to do this.

Ian   Yes you do.

Cate   I don't.

Ian   Why not? You're nervous, that's all.

> (*He starts to kiss her again.*)

Cate   I t- t- t- t- t- t- t- told you. I really like you but I
c- c- c- c- can't do this.

Ian   (*Kissing her.*) Shhh.

> (*He starts to undo her trousers.*)

> **Cate** *panics.*
> *She starts to tremble and make inarticulate crying sounds.*
> **Ian** *stops, frightened of bringing another 'fit' on.*

Ian   All right, Cate, it's all right. We don't have to do
anything.

> *He strokes her face until she has calmed down.*
> *She sucks her thumb.*
> *Then.*

Ian   That wasn't very fair.

Cate What?

Ian Leaving me hanging, making a prick of myself.

Cate I f- f- felt –

Ian Don't pity me, Cate. You don't have to fuck me 'cause I'm dying, but don't push your cunt in my face then take it away 'cause I stick my tongue out.

Cate I- I- Ian.

Ian What's the m- m- matter?

Cate I k- k- kissed you, that's all. I l- l- like you.

Ian Don't give me a hard-on if you're not going to finish me off. It hurts.

Cate I'm sorry.

Ian Can't switch it on and off like that. If I don't come my cock aches.

Cate I didn't mean it.

Ian Shit. (*He appears to be in considerable pain.*)

Cate I'm sorry. I am. I won't do it again.

> **Ian**, *apparently still in pain, takes her hand and grasps it around his penis, keeping his own hand over the top.*
> *Like this, he masturbates until he comes with some genuine pain.*
> *He releases* **Cate***'s hand and she withdraws it.*

Cate Is it better?

Ian (*Nods.*)

Cate I'm sorry.

Ian Don't worry. Can we make love tonight?

Cate No.

Ian Why not?

Cate I'm not your girlfriend any more.

Ian   Will you be my girlfriend again?

Cate   I can't.

Ian   Why not?

Cate   I told Shaun I'd be his.

Ian   Have you slept with him?

Cate   No.

Ian   Slept with me before. You're more mine than his.

Cate   I'm not.

Ian   What was that about then, wanking me off?

Cate   I d- d- d- d-

Ian   Sorry. Pressure, pressure. I love you, that's all.

Cate   You were horrible to me.

Ian   I wasn't.

Cate   Stopped phoning me, never said why.

Ian   It was difficult, Cate.

Cate   Because I haven't got a job?

Ian   No, pet, not that.

Cate   Because of my brother?

Ian   No, no, Cate. Leave it now.

Cate   That's not fair.

Ian   I said leave it.

(*He reaches for his gun.*)

There is a knock at the door.
Ian *starts, then goes to answer it.*

Ian   I'm not going to hurt you, just leave it. And keep quiet.
It'll only be Sooty after something.

Cate   Andrew.

Ian   What do you want to know a conker's name for?

Cate   I thought he was nice.

Ian   After a bit of black meat, eh? Won't do it with me but you'll go with a whodat.

Cate   You're horrible.

Ian   Cate, love, I'm trying to look after you. Stop you getting hurt.

Cate   You hurt me.

Ian   No, I love you.

Cate   Stopped loving me.

Ian   I've told you to leave that.
Now.

He kisses her passionately, then goes to the door.
When his back is turned, **Cate** *wipes her mouth.*
Ian *opens the door. There is a bottle of gin outside on a tray.*
Ian *brings it in and stands, unable to decide between gin and champagne.*

Cate   Have champagne, better for you.

Ian   Don't want it better for me.

   (*He pours himself a gin.*)

Cate   You'll die quicker.

Ian   Thanks. Don't it scare you?

Cate   What?

Ian   Death.

Cate   Whose?

Ian   Yours.

Cate   Only for Mum. She'd be unhappy if I died. And my brother.

Ian   You're young.
When I was your age –
Now.

Cate   Will you have to go to hospital?

Ian   Nothing they can do.

Cate   Does Stella know?

Ian   What would I want to tell her for?

Cate   You were married.

Ian   So?

Cate   She'd want to know.

Ian   So she can throw a party at the coven.

Cate   She wouldn't do that. What about Matthew?

Ian   What about Matthew?

Cate   Have you told him?

Ian   I'll send him an invite for the funeral.

Cate   He'll be upset.

Ian   He hates me.

Cate   He doesn't.

Ian   He fucking does.

Cate   Are you upset?

Ian   Yes. His mother's a lesbos. Am I not preferable to that?

Cate   Perhaps she's a nice person.

Ian   She don't carry a gun.

Cate   I expect that's it.

Ian   I loved Stella till she became a witch and fucked off with a dyke, and I love you, though you've got the potential.

Cate   For what?

Ian   Sucking gash.

Cate   (*Utters an inarticulate sound.*)

Ian   You ever had a fuck with a woman?

Cate   No.

Ian   You want to?

Cate   Don't think so. Have you? With a man.

Ian   You think I'm a cocksucker? You've seen me. (*He vaguely indicates his groin.*) How can you think that?

Cate   I don't. I asked. You asked me.

Ian   You dress like a lesbos. I don't dress like a cocksucker.

Cate   What do they dress like?

Ian   Hitler was wrong about the Jews who have they hurt the queers he should have gone for scum them and the wogs and fucking football fans send a bomber over Elland Road finish them off.

(*He pours champagne and toasts the idea.*)

Cate   I like football.

Ian   Why?

Cate   It's good.

Ian   And when was the last time you went to a football match?

Cate   Saturday. United beat Liverpool 2–0.

Ian   Didn't you get stabbed?

Cate   Why should I?

Ian   That's what football's about. It's not fancy footwork and scoring goals. It's tribalism.

Cate   I like it.

Ian   You would. About your level.

Cate   I go to Elland Road sometimes. Would you bomb me?

Ian   What do you want to ask a question like that for?

Cate   Would you though?

Ian   Don't be thick.

Cate   But would you?

Ian   Haven't got a bomber.

Cate   Shoot me, then. Could you do that?

Ian   Cate.

Cate   Do you think it's hard to shoot someone?

Ian   Easy as shitting blood.

Cate   Could you shoot me?

Ian   Could you shoot me stop asking that could you shoot me you could shoot me.

Cate   I don't think so.

Ian   If I hurt you.

Cate   Don't think you would.

Ian   But if.

Cate   No, you're soft.

Ian   With people I love.

(*He stares at her, considering making a pass.*)

Cate   (*Smiles at him, friendly.*)

Ian   What's this job, then?

Cate Personal Assistant.

Ian Who to?

Cate Don't know.

Ian Who did you write the letter to?

Cate Sir or madam.

Ian You have to know who you're writing to.

Cate It didn't say.

Ian How much?

Cate What?

Ian Money. How much do you get paid.

Cate Mum said it was a lot. I don't mind about that as long as I can go out sometimes.

Ian Don't despise money. You got it easy.

Cate I haven't got any money.

Ian No and you haven't got kids to bring up neither.

Cate Not yet.

Ian Don't even think about it. Who would have children. You have kids, they grow up, they hate you and you die.

Cate I don't hate Mum.

Ian You still need her.

Cate You think I'm stupid. I'm not stupid.

Ian I worry.

Cate Can look after myself.

Ian Like me.

Cate No.

Ian You hate me, don't you.

Cate   You shouldn't have that gun.

Ian   May need it.

Cate   What for?

Ian   (*Drinks.*)

Cate   Can't imagine it.

Ian   What?

Cate   You. Shooting someone. You wouldn't kill anything.

Ian   (*Drinks.*)

Cate   Have you ever shot anyone?

Ian   Your mind.

Cate   Have you though?

Ian   Leave it now, Cate.

She takes the warning.
Ian *kisses her and lights a cigarette.*

Ian   When I'm with you I can't think about anything else.
You take me to another place.

Cate   It's like that when I have a fit.

Ian   Just you.

Cate   The world don't exist, not like this.
Looks the same but –
Time slows down.
A dream I get stuck in, can't do nothing about it.
One time –

Ian   Make love to me.

Cate   Blocks out everything else.
Once –

Ian   [I'll] Make love to you.

Cate   It's like that when I touch myself.

Ian *is embarrassed.*

Cate Just before I'm wondering what it'll be like, and just after I'm thinking about the next one, but just as it happens it's lovely, I don't think of nothing else.

Ian Like the first cigarette of the day.

Cate That's bad for you though.

Ian Stop talking now, you don't know anything about it.

Cate Don't need to.

Ian Don't know nothing. That's why I love you, want to make love to you.

Cate But you can't.

Ian Why not?

Cate I don't want to.

Ian Why did you come here?

Cate You sounded unhappy.

Ian Make me happy.

Cate I can't.

Ian Please.

Cate No.

Ian Why not?

Cate Can't.

Ian Can.

Cate How?

Ian You know.

Cate Don't.

Ian Please.

Cate No.

Ian I love you.

Cate I don't love you.

Ian (*Turns away. He sees the bouquet of flowers and picks it up.*)

These are for you.

Blackout.

The sound of spring rain.

Scene Two

The same.

Very early the following morning.
Bright and sunny – it's going to be a very hot day.
The bouquet of flowers is now ripped apart and scattered around the room.

Cate *is still asleep.*
Ian *is awake, glancing through the newspapers.*

Ian *goes to the mini-bar. It is empty.*
He finds the bottle of gin under the bed and pours half of what is left into a glass.
He stands looking out of the window at the street.
He takes the first sip and is overcome with pain.
He waits for it to pass, but it doesn't. It gets worse.
Ian *clutches his side – it becomes extreme.*
He begins to cough and experiences intense pain in his chest, each cough tearing at his lung.

Cate *wakes and watches* **Ian**.

Ian *drops to his knees, puts the glass down carefully, and gives in to the pain.*
It looks very much as if he is dying.
His heart, lung, liver and kidneys are all under attack and he is making involuntary crying sounds.

Just at the moment when it seems he cannot survive this, it begins to ease.
Very slowly, the pain decreases until it has all gone.

Ian *is a crumpled heap on the floor.*

He looks up and sees **Cate** *watching him.*

Cate   Cunt.

Ian   (*Gets up slowly, picks up the glass and drinks.*
He lights his first cigarette of the day.)

I'm having a shower.

Cate   It's only six o'clock.

Ian   Want one?

Cate   Not with you.

Ian   Suit yourself. Cigarette?

Cate   (*Makes a noise of disgust.*)

They are silent.

Ian *stands, smoking and drinking neat gin.*
When he's sufficiently numbed, he comes and goes between the bedroom and bathroom, undressing and collecting discarded towels.
He stops, towel around his waist, gun in hand, and looks at **Cate**.
She is staring at him with hate.

Ian   Don't worry, I'll be dead soon.

(*He tosses the gun onto the bed.*)

Have a pop.

Cate *doesn't move.*
Ian *waits, then chuckles and goes into the bathroom.*
We hear the shower running.

Cate *stares at the gun.*
She gets up very slowly and dresses.
She packs her bag.
She picks up **Ian**'s *leather jacket and smells it.*

She rips the arms off at the seams.
She picks up his gun and examines it.
We hear **Ian** *coughing up in the bathroom.*
Cate *puts the gun down and he comes in.*
He dresses.
He looks at the gun.

Ian   No?

(*He chuckles, unloads and reloads the gun and tucks it in his holster.*)

We're one, yes?

Cate   (*Sneers.*)

Ian   We're one.
Coming down for breakfast? It's paid for.

Cate   Choke on it.

Ian   Sarky little tart this morning, aren't we?

He picks up his jacket and puts one arm through a hole.
He stares at the damage, then looks at **Cate**.
A beat, then she goes for him, slapping him around the head hard and fast.
He wrestles her onto the bed, her still kicking, punching and biting.
She takes the gun from his holster and points it at his groin.
He backs off rapidly.

Ian   Easy, easy, that's a loaded gun.

Cate   I d- d- d- d- d- d- d- d- d-

Ian   Catie, come on.

Cate   d- d- d- d- d- d- d- d- d- d-

Ian   You don't want an accident. Think about your mum.
And your brother. What would they think?

Cate   I d- d- d- d- d- d- d- d- d- d- d- d- d-

Cate *trembles and starts gasping for air.*
She faints.

Ian *goes to her, takes the gun and puts it back in the holster.*
Then lies her on the bed on her back.
He puts the gun to her head, lies between her legs, and simulates sex.
As he comes, **Cate** *sits bolt upright with a shout.*
Ian *moves away, unsure what to do, pointing the gun at her from behind.*
She laughs hysterically, as before, but doesn't stop.
She laughs and laughs and laughs until she isn't laughing any more, she's crying her heart out.
She collapses again and lies still.

Ian Cate? Catie?

Ian *puts the gun away.*
He kisses her and she comes round.
She stares at him.

Ian You back?

Cate Liar.

Ian *doesn't know if this means yes or no, so he just waits.*
Cate *closes her eyes for a few seconds, then opens them.*

Ian Cate?

Cate Want to go home now.

Ian It's not even seven. There won't be a train.

Cate I'll wait at the station.

Ian It's raining.

Cate It's not.

Ian Want you to stay here. Till after breakfast at least.

Cate No.

Ian Cate. After breakfast.

Cate No.

Ian (*Locks the door and pockets the key.*)

   I love you.

Cate   I don't want to stay.

Ian   Please.

Cate   Don't want to.

Ian   You make me feel safe.

Cate   Nothing to be scared of.

Ian   I'll order breakfast.

Cate   Not hungry.

Ian   (*Lights a cigarette.*)

Cate   How can you smoke on an empty stomach?

Ian   It's not empty. There's gin in it.

Cate   Why can't I go home?

Ian   (*Thinks.*)

It's too dangerous.

Outside, a car backfires – there is an enormous bang.
Ian *throws himself flat on the floor.*

Cate   (*Laughs.*)

It's only a car.

Ian   You. You're fucking thick.

Cate   I'm not. You're scared of things when there's nothing
to be scared of. What's thick about not being scared of
cars?

Ian   I'm not scared of cars. I'm scared of dying.

Cate   A car won't kill you. Not from out there.
Not unless you ran out in front of it.

(*She kisses him.*)

What's scaring you?

Ian   Thought it was a gun.

Cate   (*Kisses his neck.*)

Who'd have a gun?

Ian   Me.

Cate   (*Undoes his shirt.*)

You're in here.

Ian   Someone like me.

Cate   (*Kisses his chest.*)

Why would they shoot at you?

Ian   Revenge.

Cate   (*Runs her hands down his back.*)

Ian   For things I've done.

Cate   (*Massages his neck.*)

Tell me.

Ian   Tapped my phone.

Cate   (*Kisses the back of his neck.*)

Ian   Talk to people and I know I'm being listened to. I'm sorry I stopped calling you but –

Cate   (*Strokes his stomach and kisses between his shoulder blades.*)

Ian   Got angry when you said you loved me, talking soft on the phone, people listening to that.

Cate   (*Kisses his back.*)

Tell me.

Ian   In before you know it.

Cate   (*Licks his back.*)

Ian   Signed the Official Secrets Act, shouldn't be telling you this.

Cate   (*Claws and scratches his back.*)

Ian   Don't want to get you into trouble.

Cate   (*Bites his back.*)

Ian   Think they're trying to kill me. Served my purpose.

Cate   (*Pushes him onto his back.*)

Ian   Done the jobs they asked. Because I love this land.

Cate   (*Sucks his nipples.*)

Ian   Stood at stations, listened to conversations and given the nod.

Cate   (*Undoes his trousers.*)

Ian   Driving jobs. Picking people up, disposing of bodies, the lot.

Cate   (*Begins to perform oral sex on* **Ian**.)

Ian   Said you were dangerous.

So I stopped.

Didn't want you in any danger.

But

Had to call you again

Missed

This

Now

I do

The real job

I

Am

A

Killer

On the word 'killer' he comes.
As soon as **Cate** *hears the word she bites his penis as hard as she can.*
Ian*'s cry of pleasure turns into a scream of pain.*
He tries to pull away but **Cate** *holds on with her teeth.*
He hits her and she lets go.
Ian *lies in pain, unable to speak.*
Cate *spits frantically, trying to get every trace of him out of her mouth.*
She goes to the bathroom and we hear her cleaning her teeth.
Ian *examines himself. He is still in one piece.*
Cate *returns.*

Cate   You should resign.

Ian   Don't work like that.

Cate   Will they come here?

Ian   I don't know.

Cate   (*Begins to panic.*)

Ian   Don't start that again.

Cate   I c- c- c- c- c-

Ian   Cate, I'll shoot you myself you don't stop.
I told you because I love you, not to scare you.

Cate   You don't.

Ian   Don't argue I do. And you love me.

Cate   No more.

Ian   Loved me last night.

Cate   I didn't want to do it.

Ian   Thought you liked that.

Cate   No.

Ian   Made enough noise.

Cate   It was hurting.

Ian Went down on Stella all the time, didn't hurt her.

Cate You bit me. It's still bleeding.

Ian Is that what this is all about?

Cate You're cruel.

Ian Don't be stupid.

Cate Stop calling me that.

Ian You sleep with someone holding hands and kissing you wank me off then say we can't fuck get into bed but don't want me to touch you what's wrong with you Joey?

Cate I'm not. You're cruel. I wouldn't shoot someone.

Ian Pointed it at me.

Cate Wouldn't shoot.

Ian It's my job. I love this country. I won't see it destroyed by slag.

Cate It's wrong to kill.

Ian Planting bombs and killing little kiddies, that's wrong. That's what they do. Kids like your brother.

Cate It's wrong.

Ian Yes, it is.

Cate No. You. Doing that.

Ian When are you going to grow up?

Cate I don't believe in killing.

Ian You'll learn.

Cate No I won't.

Ian Can't always be taking it backing down letting them think they've got a right turn the other cheek SHIT

some things are worth more than that have to be
protected from shite.

Cate I used to love you.

Ian What's changed?

Cate You.

Ian No. Now you see me. That's all.

Cate You're a nightmare.

She shakes.
Ian *watches a while, then hugs her.*
She is still shaking so he hugs tightly to stop her.

Cate That hurts.

Ian Sorry.

He hugs her less tightly.
He has a coughing fit.
He spits into his handkerchief and waits for the pain to subside.
Then he lights a cigarette.

Ian How you feeling?

Cate I ache.

Ian (*Nods.*)

Cate Everywhere.
I stink of you.

Ian You want a bath?

Cate *begins to cough and retch.*
She puts her fingers down her throat and produces a hair.
She holds it up and looks at **Ian** *in disgust. She spits.*
Ian *goes into the bathroom and turns on one of the bath taps.*
Cate *stares out of the window.*
Ian *returns.*

Cate Looks like there's a war on.

Ian   (*Doesn't look.*)

>   Turning into Wogland.
>   You coming to Leeds again?

Cate   Twenty-sixth.

Ian   Will you come and see me?

Cate   I'm going to the football.

She goes to the bathroom.
Ian *picks up the phone.*

Ian   Two English breakfasts, son.

He finishes the remainder of the gin.
Cate *returns.*

Cate   I can't piss. It's just blood.

Ian   Drink lots of water.

Cate   Or shit. It hurts.

Ian   It'll heal.

There is a knock at the door. They both jump.

Cate   DON'T ANSWER IT DON'T ANSWER IT
DON'T ANSWER IT

She dives on the bed and puts her head under the pillow.

Ian   Cate, shut up.

He pulls the pillow off and puts the gun to her head.

Cate   Do it. Go on, shoot me. Can't be no worse than what
you've done already. Shoot me if you want, then turn
it on yourself and do the world a favour.

Ian   (*Stares at her.*)

Cate   I'm not scared of you, Ian. Go on.

Ian   (*Gets off her.*)

Cate   (*Laughs.*)

Ian Answer the door and suck the cunt's cock.

Cate tries to open the door. It is locked.
Ian throws the key at her.
She opens the door.
The breakfasts are outside on a tray. She brings them in.
Ian locks the door.
Cate stares at the food.

Cate Sausages. Bacon.

Ian Sorry. Forgot. Swap your meat for my tomatoes and mushrooms. And toast.

Cate (*Begins to retch.*)

   The smell.

Ian takes a sausage off the plate and stuffs it in his mouth and keeps a rasher of bacon in his hand.
He puts the tray of food under the bed with a towel over it.

Ian Will you stay another day?

Cate I'm having a bath and going home.

She picks up her bag and goes into the bathroom, closing the door.
We hear the other bath tap being turned on.
There are two loud knocks at the outer door.
Ian draws his gun, goes to the door and listens.
The door is tried from outside. It is locked.
There are two more loud knocks.

Ian Who's there?

Silence.
Then two more loud knocks.

Ian Who's there?

Silence.
Then two more knocks.
Ian looks at the door.
Then he knocks twice.
Silence.

Then two more knocks from outside.

Ian *thinks.*
Then he knocks three times.

Silence.
Three knocks from outside.

Ian *knocks once.*
One knock from outside.

Ian *knocks twice.*
Two knocks.

Ian *puts his gun back in the holster and unlocks the door.*

Ian   (*Under his breath.*) Speak the Queen's English fucking
nigger.

He opens the door.
*Outside is a **Soldier** with a sniper's rifle.*
***Ian** tries to push the door shut and draw his revolver.*
*The **Soldier** pushes the door open and takes **Ian***'s gun*
easily.
The two stand, both surprised, staring at each other.
Eventually.

Soldier   What's that?

Ian *looks down and realises he is still holding a rasher of bacon.*

Ian   Pig.

*The **Soldier** holds out his hand.*
***Ian** gives him the bacon and he eats it quickly, rind and all.*
*The **Soldier** wipes his mouth.*

Soldier   Got any more?

Ian   No.

Soldier   Got any more?

Ian   I –
No.

Soldier   Got any more?

Ian   (*Points to the tray under the bed.*)

> The **Soldier** *bends down carefully, never taking his eyes or rifle off*
> **Ian**, *and takes the tray from under the bed.*
> *He straightens up and glances down at the food.*

Soldier   Two.

Ian   I was hungry.

Soldier   I bet.

> The **Soldier** *sits on the edge of the bed and very quickly devours both*
> *breakfasts.*
> *He sighs with relief and burps.*
> *He nods towards the bathroom.*

Soldier   She in there?

Ian   Who?

Soldier   I can smell the sex.

> (*He begins to search the room.*)

> You a journalist?

Ian   I –

Soldier   Passport.

Ian   What for?

Soldier   (*Looks at him.*)

Ian   In the jacket.

> The **Soldier** *is searching a chest of drawers.*
> *He finds a pair of* **Cate**'s *knickers and holds them up.*

Soldier   Hers?

Ian   (*Doesn't answer.*)

Soldier   Or yours.

> (*He closes his eyes and rubs them gently over his face, smelling*
> *with pleasure.*)

What's she like?

Ian   (*Doesn't answer.*)

Soldier   Is she soft?
Is she − ?

Ian   (*Doesn't answer.*)

> The **Soldier** *puts* **Cate***'s knickers in his pocket and goes to the bathroom.*
> *He knocks on the door. No answer.*
> *He tries the door. It is locked.*
> *He forces it and goes in.*
> **Ian** *waits, in a panic.*
> *We hear the bath taps being turned off.*
> **Ian** *looks out of the window.*

Ian   Jesus Lord.

> The **Soldier** *returns.*

Soldier   Gone. Taking a risk. Lot of bastard soldiers out there.

> **Ian** *looks in the bathroom.* **Cate** *isn't there.*
> *The* **Soldier** *looks in* **Ian***'s jacket pockets and takes his keys, wallet and passport.*

Soldier   (*Looks at* **Ian***'s press card.*)

Ian Jones.
Journalist.

Ian   Oi.

Soldier   Oi.

> *They stare at each other.*

Ian   If you've come to shoot me −

Soldier   (*Reaches out to touch* **Ian***'s face but stops short of physical contact.*)

Ian   You taking the piss?

Soldier   Me?

>   (*He smiles.*)

>   Our town now.

>   (*He stands on the bed and urinates over the pillows.*)

Ian *is disgusted.*

There is a blinding light, then a huge explosion.

Blackout.

The sound of summer rain.

Scene Three

The hotel has been blasted by a mortar bomb.

There is a large hole in one of the walls, and everything is covered in dust which is still falling.

The **Soldier** *is unconscious, rifle still in hand.*
He has dropped **Ian***'s gun which lies between them.*

Ian *lies very still, eyes open.*

Ian   Mum?

Silence.
The **Soldier** *wakes and turns his eyes and rifle on* **Ian** *with the minimum possible movement.*
He instinctively runs his free hand over his limbs and body to check that he is still in one piece. He is.

Soldier   The drink.

Ian *looks around. There is a bottle of gin lying next to him with the lid off.*
He holds it up to the light.

Ian   Empty.

Soldier   (*Takes the bottle and drinks the last mouthful.*)

Ian   (*Chuckles.*)

Worse than me.

*The **Soldier** holds the bottle up and shakes it over his mouth, catching any remaining drops.*

***Ian** finds his cigarettes in his shirt pocket and lights up.*

Soldier   Give us a cig.

Ian   Why?

Soldier   'Cause I've got a gun and you haven't.

***Ian** considers the logic.*
Then takes a single cigarette out of the packet and tosses it at the **Soldier**.
*The **Soldier** picks up the cigarette and puts it in his mouth.*
*He looks at **Ian**, waiting for a light.*
***Ian** holds out his cigarette.*
*The **Soldier** leans forward, touching the tip of his cigarette against the lit one, eyes always on **Ian**.*
He smokes.

Soldier   Never met an Englishman with a gun before, most of them don't know what a gun is. You a soldier?

Ian   Of sorts.

Soldier   Which side, if you can remember.

Ian   Don't know what the sides are here.
Don't know where . . .

(*He trails off confused, and looks at the **Soldier**.*)

Think I might be drunk.

Soldier   No. It's real.

(*He picks up the revolver and examines it.*)

Come to fight for us?

Ian   No, I –

Soldier   No, course not. English.

Ian   I'm Welsh.

Soldier   Sound English, fucking accent.

Ian   I live there.

Soldier   Foreigner?

Ian   English and Welsh is the same. British. I'm not an import.

Soldier   What's fucking Welsh, never heard of it.

Ian   Come over from God knows where have their kids and call them English they're not English born in England don't make you English.

Soldier   Welsh as in Wales?

Ian   It's attitude.

(*He turns away.*)

Look at the state of my fucking jacket. The bitch.

Soldier   Your girlfriend did that, angry was she?

Ian   She's not my girlfriend.

Soldier   What, then?

Ian   Mind your fucking own.

Soldier   Haven't been here long have you.

Ian   So?

Soldier   Learn some manners, Ian.

Ian   Don't call me that.

Soldier   What shall I call you?

Ian   Nothing.

Silence.

The **Soldier** *looks at* **Ian** *for a very long time, saying nothing.*
Ian *is uncomfortable.*
Eventually.

Ian   What?

Soldier   Nothing.

Silence.
Ian *is uneasy again.*

Ian   My name's Ian.

Soldier   I
Am
Dying to make love
Ian

Ian   (*Looks at him.*)

Soldier   You got a girlfriend?

Ian   (*Doesn't answer.*)

Soldier   I have.
Col.
Fucking beautiful.

Ian   Cate –

Soldier   Close my eyes and think about her.
She's –
She's –
She's –
She's –
She's –
She's –
She's –
When was the last time you – ?

Ian   (*Looks at him.*)

Soldier   When? I know it was recent, smell it, remember.

Ian   Last night. I think.

Soldier Good?

Ian Don't know. I was pissed. Probably not.

Soldier Three of us –

Ian Don't tell me.

Soldier Went to a house just outside town. All gone. Apart from a small boy hiding in the corner. One of the others took him outside. Lay him on the ground and shot him through the legs. Heard crying in the basement. Went down. Three men and four women. Called the others. They held the men while I fucked the women. Youngest was twelve. Didn't cry, just lay there. Turned her over and –
Then she cried. Made her lick me clean. Closed my eyes and thought of –
Shot her father in the mouth. Brothers shouted. Hung them from the ceiling by their testicles.

Ian Charming.

Soldier Never done that?

Ian No.

Soldier Sure?

Ian I wouldn't forget.

Soldier You would.

Ian Couldn't sleep with myself.

Soldier What about your wife?

Ian I'm divorced.

Soldier Didn't you ever –

Ian No.

Soldier What about that girl locked herself in the bathroom.

Ian (*Doesn't answer.*)

Soldier   Ah.

Ian   You did four in one go, I've only ever done one.

Soldier   You killed her?

Ian   (*Makes a move for his gun.*)

Soldier   Don't, I'll have to shoot you. Then I'd be lonely.

Ian   Course I haven't.

Soldier   Why not, don't seem to like her very much.

Ian   I do.
She's . . . a woman.

Soldier   So?

Ian   I've never –
It's not –

Soldier   What?

Ian   (*Doesn't answer.*)

Soldier   Thought you were a soldier.

Ian   Not like that.

Soldier   Not like that, they're all like that.

Ian   My job –

Soldier   Even me. Have to be.
My girl –
Not going back to her. When I go back.
She's dead, see. Fucking bastard soldier, he –

He stops.
Silence.

Ian   I'm sorry.

Soldier   Why?

Ian   It's terrible.

Soldier   What is?

Ian   Losing someone, a woman, like that.

Soldier   You know, do you?

Ian   I –

Soldier   Like what?

Ian   Like –
You said –
A soldier –

Soldier   You're a soldier.

Ian   I haven't –

Soldier   What if you were ordered to?

Ian   Can't imagine it.

Soldier   Imagine it.

Ian   (*Imagines it.*)

Soldier   In the line of duty.
For your country.
Wales.

Ian   (*Imagines harder.*)

Soldier   Foreign slag.

Ian   (*Imagines harder. Looks sick.*)

Soldier   Would you?

Ian   (*Nods.*)

Soldier   How.

Ian   Quickly. Back of the head. Bam.

Soldier   That's all.

Ian   It's enough.

Soldier   You think?

Ian   Yes.

Soldier   You never killed anyone.

Ian   Fucking have.

Soldier   No.

Ian   Don't you fucking –

Soldier   Couldn't talk like this. You'd know.

Ian   Know what?

Soldier   Exactly. You don't know.

Ian   Know fucking what?

Soldier   Stay in the dark.

Ian   What? Fucking what? What don't I know?

Soldier   You think –

>   (*He stops and smiles.*)

>   I broke a woman's neck. Stabbed up between her legs, on the fifth stab snapped her spine.

Ian   (*Looks sick.*)

Soldier   You couldn't do that.

Ian   No.

Soldier   You never killed.

Ian   Not like that.

Soldier   Not
Like
That

Ian   I'm not a torturer.

Soldier   You're close to them, gun to head. Tie them up, tell them what you're going to do to them, make them wait for it, then ... what?

Ian   Shoot them.

Soldier You haven't got a clue.

Ian What then?

Soldier You never fucked a man before you killed him?

Ian No.

Soldier Or after?

Ian Course not.

Soldier Why not?

Ian What for, I'm not queer.

Soldier Col, they buggered her. Cut her throat. Hacked her
ears and nose off, nailed them to the front door.

Ian Enough.

Soldier Ever seen anything like that?

Ian Stop.

Soldier Not in photos?

Ian Never.

Soldier Some journalist, that's your job.

Ian What?

Soldier Proving it happened. I'm here, got no choice. But
you. You should be telling people.

Ian No one's interested.

Soldier You can do something, for me –

Ian No.

Soldier Course you can.

Ian I can't do anything.

Soldier Try.

Ian I write ... stories. That's all. Stories. This isn't a story anyone wants to hear.

Soldier Why not?

Ian (*Takes one of the newspapers from the bed and reads.*)

'Kinky car dealer Richard Morris drove two teenage prostitutes into the country, tied them naked to fences and whipped them with a belt before having sex. Morris, from Sheffield, was jailed for three years for unlawful sexual intercourse with one of the girls, aged thirteen.'

(*He tosses the paper away.*)

Stories.

Soldier Doing to them what they done to us, what good is that? At home I'm clean. Like it never happened. Tell them you saw me.
Tell them ... you saw me.

Ian It's not my job.

Soldier Whose is it?

Ian I'm a home journalist, for Yorkshire. I don't cover foreign affairs.

Soldier Foreign affairs, what you doing here?

Ian I do other stuff. Shootings and rapes and kids getting fiddled by queer priests and schoolteachers. Not soldiers screwing each other for a patch of land. It has to be ... personal. Your girlfriend, she's a story. Soft and clean. Not you. Filthy, like the wogs. No joy in a story about blacks who gives a shit? Why bring you to light?

Soldier You don't know fuck all about me.
I went to school.
I made love with Col.

Bastards killed her, now I'm here.
Now I'm here.

(*He pushes the rifle in* **Ian***'s face.*)

Turn over, Ian.

Ian   Why?

Soldier   Going to fuck you.

Ian   No.

Soldier   Kill you then.

Ian   Fine.

Soldier   See. Rather be shot than fucked and shot.

Ian   Yes.

Soldier   And now you agree with anything I say.

He kisses **Ian** *very tenderly on the lips.*
They stare at each other.

Soldier   You smell like her. Same cigarettes.

The **Soldier** *turns* **Ian** *over with one hand.*
He holds the revolver to **Ian***'s head with the other.*
He pulls down **Ian***'s trousers, undoes his own and rapes him – eyes*
closed and smelling **Ian***'s hair.*
The **Soldier** *is crying his heart out.*

Ian*'s face registers pain but he is silent.*

When the **Soldier** *has finished he pulls up his trousers and pushes the*
revolver up **Ian***'s anus.*

Soldier   Bastard pulled the trigger on Col.
What's it like?

Ian   (*Tries to answer. He can't.*)

Soldier   (*Withdraws the gun and sits next to* **Ian**.)

You never fucked by a man before?

Ian   (*Doesn't answer.*)

Soldier   Didn't think so. It's nothing. Saw thousands of people packing into trucks like pigs trying to leave town. Women threw their babies on board hoping someone would look after them. Crushing each other to death. Insides of people's heads came out of their eyes. Saw a child most of his face blown off, young girl I fucked hand up inside her trying to claw my liquid out, starving man eating his dead wife's leg. Gun was born here and won't die. Can't get tragic about your arse. Don't think your Welsh arse is different to any other arse I fucked. Sure you haven't got any more food, I'm fucking starving.

Ian   Are you going to kill me?

Soldier   Always covering your own arse.

The **Soldier** *grips* **Ian**'*s head in his hands.*

He puts his mouth over one of **Ian**'*s eyes, sucks it out, bites it off and eats it.*

He does the same to the other eye.

Soldier   He ate her eyes.
          Poor bastard.
          Poor love.
          Poor fucking bastard.

Blackout.

The sound of autumn rain.

Scene Four

The same.

The **Soldier** *lies close to* **Ian**, *the revolver in his hand. He has blown his own brain out.*

Cate *enters through the bathroom door, soaking wet and carrying a baby.*
She steps over the **Soldier** *with a glance.*
Then she sees **Ian**.

Cate   You're a nightmare.

Ian   Cate?

Cate   It won't stop.

Ian   Catie? You here?

Cate   Everyone in town is crying.

Ian   Touch me.

Cate   Soldiers have taken over.

Ian   They've won?

Cate   Most people gave up.

Ian   You seen Matthew?

Cate   No.

Ian   Will you tell him for me?

Cate   He isn't here.

Ian   Tell him –
Tell him –

Cate   No.

Ian   Don't know what to tell him.
I'm cold.
Tell him –
You here?

Cate   A woman gave me her baby.

Ian   You come for me, Catie? Punish me or rescue me makes no difference I love you Cate tell him for me do it for me touch me Cate.

Cate   Don't know what to do with it.

Ian   I'm cold.

Cate   Keeps crying.

Ian   Tell him –

Cate   I CAN'T.

Ian   Will you stay with me, Cate?

Cate   No.

Ian   Why not?

Cate   I have to go back soon.

Ian   Shaun know what we did?

Cate   No.

Ian   Better tell him.

Cate   No.

Ian   He'll know. Even if you don't.

Cate   How?

Ian   Smell it. Soiled goods. Don't want it, not when you can have someone clean.

Cate   What's happened to your eyes?

Ian   I need you to stay, Cate. Won't be for long.

Cate   Do you know about babies?

Ian   No.

Cate   What about Matthew?

Ian   He's twenty-four.

Cate   When he was born.

Ian   They shit and cry. Hopeless.

Cate   Bleeding.

Ian   Will you touch me?

Cate No.

Ian So I know you're here.

Cate You can hear me.

Ian Won't hurt you, I promise.

Cate (*Goes to him slowly and touches the top of his head.*)

Ian Help me.

Cate (*Strokes his hair.*)

Ian Be dead soon anyway, Cate.
And it hurts.
Help me to –
Help me –
Finish
It

Cate (*Withdraws her hand.*)

Ian Catie?

Cate Got to get something for Baby to eat.

Ian Won't find anything.

Cate May as well look.

Ian Fucking bastards ate it all.

Cate It'll die.

Ian Needs its mother's milk.

Cate Ian.

Ian Stay.
Nowhere to go, where are you going to go?
Bloody dangerous on your own, look at me.
Safer here with me.

Cate *considers.*
Then sits down with the baby some distance from **Ian**.
He relaxes when he hears her sit.

Cate *rocks the baby.*

Ian   Not as bad as all that, am I?

Cate   (*Looks at him.*)

Ian   Will you help me, Catie?

Cate   How.

Ian   Find my gun?

> **Cate** *thinks.*
> *Then gets up and searches around, baby in arms.*
> *She sees the revolver in the **Soldier**'s hand and stares at it for some time.*

Ian   Found it?

Cate   No.

> *She takes the revolver from the **Soldier** and fiddles with it.*
> *It springs open and she stares in at the bullets.*
> *She removes them and closes the gun.*

Ian   That it?

Cate   Yes.

Ian   Can I have it?

Cate   I don't think so.

Ian   Catie.

Cate   What?

Ian   Come on.

Cate   Don't tell me what to do.

Ian   I'm not, love. Can you keep that baby quiet.

Cate   It's not doing anything. It's hungry.

Ian   We're all bloody hungry, don't shoot myself I'll starve to death.

Cate   It's wrong to kill yourself.

Ian   No it's not.

Cate   God wouldn't like it.

Ian   There isn't one.

Cate   How do you know?

Ian   No God. No Father Christmas. No fairies. No Narnia. No fucking nothing.

Cate   Got to be something.

Ian   Why?

Cate   Doesn't make sense otherwise.

Ian   Don't be fucking stupid, doesn't make sense anyway. No reason for there to be a God just because it would be better if there was.

Cate   Thought you didn't want to die.

Ian   I can't see.

Cate   My brother's got blind friends. You can't give up.

Ian   Why not?

Cate   It's weak.

Ian   I know you want to punish me, trying to make me live.

Cate   I don't.

Ian   Course you fucking do, I would. There's people I'd love to suffer but they don't, they die and that's it.

Cate   What if you're wrong?

Ian   I'm not.

Cate   But if.

Ian   I've seen dead people. They're dead. They're not somewhere else, they're dead.

Cate   What about people who've seen ghosts?

Ian   What about them? Imagining it. Or making it up or wishing the person was still alive.

Cate   People who've died and come back say they've seen tunnels and lights –

Ian   Can't die and come back. That's not dying, it's fainting. When you die, it's the end.

Cate   I believe in God.

Ian   Everything's got a scientific explanation.

Cate   No.

Ian   Give me my gun.

Cate   What are you going to do?

Ian   I won't hurt you.

Cate   I know.

Ian   End it.
        Got to, Cate, I'm ill.
        Just speeding it up a bit.

Cate   (*Thinks hard.*)

Ian   Please.

Cate   (*Gives him the gun.*)

Ian   (*Takes the gun and puts it in his mouth.
        He takes it out again.*)

        Don't stand behind me.

*He puts the gun back in his mouth.
He pulls the trigger. The gun clicks, empty.
He shoots again. And again and again and again.
He takes the gun out of his mouth.*

Ian   Fuck.

Cate   Fate, see. You're not meant to do it. God –

Ian   The cunt.

(*He throws the gun away in despair.*)

Cate   (*Rocks the baby and looks down at it.*)

Oh no.

Ian   What.

Cate   It's dead.

Ian   Lucky bastard.

Cate   (*Bursts out laughing, unnaturally, hysterically, uncontrollably. She laughs and laughs and laughs and laughs and laughs.*)

Blackout.

The sound of heavy winter rain.

Scene Five

The same.

Cate *is burying the baby under the floor.*

She looks around and finds two pieces of wood.
She rips the lining out of **Ian***'s jacket and binds the wood together in a cross which she sticks into the floor.*
She collects a few of the scattered flowers and places them under the cross.

Cate   I don't know her name.

Ian   Don't matter. No one's going to visit.

Cate   I was supposed to look after her.

Ian   Can bury me next to her soon. Dance on my grave.

Cate   Don't feel no pain or know nothing you shouldn't know –

Ian   Cate?

Cate   Shh.

Ian   What you doing?

Cate   Praying. Just in case.

Ian   Will you pray for me?

Cate   No.

Ian   When I'm dead, not now.

Cate   No point when you're dead.

Ian   You're praying for her.

Cate   She's baby.

Ian   So?

Cate   Innocent.

Ian   Can't you forgive me?

Cate   Don't see bad things or go bad places –

Ian   She's dead, Cate.

Cate   Or meet anyone who'll do bad things.

Ian   She won't, Cate, she's dead.

Cate   Amen.

(*She starts to leave.*)

Ian   Where you going?

Cate   I'm hungry.

Ian   Cate, it's dangerous. There's no food.

Cate   Can get some off a soldier.

Ian   How?

Cate   (*Doesn't answer.*)

Ian   Don't do that.

Cate   Why not?

Ian   That's not you.

Cate   I'm hungry.

Ian   I know so am I.
But.
I'd rather –
It's not –
Please, Cate.
I'm blind.

Cate   I'm hungry.

  (*She goes.*)

Ian   Cate? Catie?
If you get some food –
Fuck.

Darkness.
Light.

Ian *masturbating.*

Ian   cunt cunt cunt cunt cunt cunt cunt cunt cunt cunt cunt

Darkness.
Light.

Ian *strangling himself with his bare hands.*

Darkness.
Light.

Ian *shitting.*
And then trying to clean it up with newspaper.

Darkness.
Light.

Ian *laughing hysterically.*

Darkness.
Light.

Ian *having a nightmare.*

Darkness.
Light.

Ian *crying, huge bloody tears.*
He is hugging the **Soldier***'s body for comfort.*

Darkness.
Light.

Ian *lying very still, weak with hunger.*

Darkness.
Light.

Ian *tears the cross out of the ground, rips up the floor and lifts the baby's body out.*

He eats the baby.

He puts the remains back in the baby's blanket and puts the bundle back in the hole.
A beat, then he climbs in after it and lies down, head poking out of the floor.

He dies with relief.

It starts to rain on him, coming through the roof.

Eventually.

Ian   Shit.

Cate *enters carrying some bread, a large sausage and a bottle of gin. There is blood seeping from between her legs.*

Cate   You're sitting under a hole.

Ian   I know.

Cate   Get wet.

Ian   Aye.

Cate   Stupid bastard.

She pulls a sheet off the bed and wraps it around her.

*She sits next to **Ian**'s head.*

She eats her fill of the sausage and bread, then washes it down with gin.

Ian *listens.*

*She feeds **Ian** with the remaining food.*

*She pours gin in **Ian**'s mouth.*

*She finishes feeding **Ian** and sits apart from him, huddled for warmth.*

She drinks the gin.
She sucks her thumb.

Silence.

It rains.

Ian   Thank you.

Blackout.

Phaedra's Love

My grateful thanks to Vincent O'Connell, Mel Kenyon and New Dramatists (New York), without whose support I could not have written this play.

For Simon, Jo and Elana.
With love.

Phaedra's Love was first performed at the Gate Theatre, London, on 15 May 1996. The cast was as follows:

Hippolytus	Cas Harkins
Phaedra	Philippa Williams
Strophe	Catherine Cusack
Doctor/Priest/Theseus	Andrew Maud
Man 1	Giles Ward
Man 2	Paolo De Paola
Woman 1	Catherine Neal
Woman 2	Diana Penny
Policeman	Andrew Scott

Directed by Sarah Kane
Designed by Vian Curtis

Characters

Hippolytus	*Crowd including:*
Doctor	**Man 1**
Phaedra	**Woman 1**
Strophe	**Child**
Priest	**Woman 2**
Theseus	**Man 2**
	Policeman 1
	Policeman 2

Author's note

Punctuation is used to indicate delivery, not to conform to the rules of grammar.

A stroke (/) marks the point of interruption in overlapping dialogue.

Words in square brackets [ ] are not spoken, but have been included in the text to clarify meaning.

Stage directions in brackets ( ) function as lines.

Editor's note

This edition of *Phaedra's Love*, first reprinted in 2000, incorporates minor revisions made to the original text by Sarah Kane shortly before her death. It should therefore be regarded as the definitive version in all respects.

Scene One

A royal palace.

Hippolytus *sits in a darkened room watching television.*
He is sprawled on a sofa surrounded by expensive electronic toys,
empty crisp and sweet packets, and a scattering of used socks and
underwear.
He is eating a hamburger, his eyes fixed on the flickering light of a
Hollywood film.
He sniffs.
He feels a sneeze coming on and rubs his nose to stop it.
It still irritates him.
He looks around the room and picks up a sock.
He examines the sock carefully then blows his nose on it.
He throws the sock back on the floor and continues to eat the hamburger.
The film becomes particularly violent.
Hippolytus *watches impassively.*
He picks up another sock, examines it and discards it.
He picks up another, examines it and decides it's fine.
He puts his penis into the sock and masturbates until he comes without
a flicker of pleasure.
He takes off the sock and throws it on the floor.
He begins another hamburger.

Scene Two

Doctor   He's depressed.

Phaedra   I know.

Doctor   He should change his diet. He can't live on
hamburgers and peanut butter.

Phaedra   I know.

Doctor   And wash his clothes occasionally. He smells.

Phaedra   I know. I told you this.

Doctor   What does he do all day?

Phaedra   Sleep.

Doctor   When he gets up.

Phaedra   Watch films. And have sex.

Doctor   He goes out?

Phaedra   No. He phones people. They come round.
They have sex and leave.

Doctor   Women?

Phaedra   There's nothing gay about Hippolytus.

Doctor   He should tidy his room and get some exercise.

Phaedra   My mother could tell me this. I thought you might
help.

Doctor   He has to help himself.

Phaedra   How much do we pay you?

Doctor   There's nothing clinically wrong. If he stays in
bed till four he's bound to feel low. He needs a
hobby.

Phaedra   He's got hobbies.

Doctor   Does he have sex with you?

Phaedra   I'm sorry?

Doctor   Does he have sex with you?

Phaedra   I'm his stepmother. We are royal.

Doctor   I don't mean to be rude, but who are these people
he has sex with? Does he pay them?

Phaedra   I really don't know.

Doctor   He must pay them.

Phaedra   He's very popular.

Doctor   Why?

Phaedra   He's funny.

Doctor   Are you in love with him?

Phaedra   I'm married to his father.

Doctor   Does he have friends?

Phaedra   He's a prince.

Doctor   But does he have friends?

Phaedra   Why don't you ask him?

Doctor   I did. I'm asking you. Does he have friends?

Phaedra   Of course.

Doctor   Who?

Phaedra   Did you actually talk to him?

Doctor   He didn't say much.

Phaedra   I'm his friend. He talks to me.

Doctor   What about?

Phaedra   Everything.

Doctor   (*Looks at her.*)

Phaedra   We're very close.

Doctor   I see. And what do you think?

Phaedra   I think my son is ill. I think you should help. I think after six years training and thirty years experience the royal doctor should come up with something better than he has to lose weight.

Doctor   Who looks after things while your husband is away?

Phaedra   Me. My daughter.

Doctor   When is he coming back?

Phaedra   I've no idea.

Doctor   Are you still in love with him?

Phaedra   Of course. I haven't seen him since we married.

Doctor   You must be very lonely.

Phaedra   I have my children.

Doctor   Perhaps your son is missing his father.

Phaedra   I doubt it.

Doctor   Perhaps he's missing his real mother.

Phaedra   (*Looks at him.*)

Doctor   That's not a reflection on your abilities as a substitute, but there is, after all, no blood between you. I'm merely speculating.

Phaedra   Quite.

Doctor   Although he's a little old to be feeling orphaned.

Phaedra   I didn't ask you to speculate. I asked for a diagnosis. And treatment.

Doctor   He's bound to be feeling low, it's his birthday.

Phaedra   He's been like this for months.

Doctor   There's nothing wrong with him medically.

Phaedra   Medically?

Doctor   He's just very unpleasant. And therefore incurable. I'm sorry.

Phaedra   I don't know what to do.

Doctor   Get over him.

Scene Three

    Strophe *is working.*
    Phaedra *enters.*

Strophe   Mother.

Phaedra   Go away fuck off don't touch me don't talk to me stay with me.

Strophe   What's wrong?

Phaedra   Nothing. Nothing at all.

Strophe   I can tell.

Phaedra   Have you ever thought, thought your heart would break?

Strophe   No.

Phaedra   Wished you could cut open your chest tear it out to stop the pain?

Strophe   That would kill you.

Phaedra   This is killing me.

Strophe   No. Just feels like it.

Phaedra   A spear in my side, burning.

Strophe   Hippolytus.

Phaedra   (*Screams.*)

Strophe   You're in love with him.

Phaedra   (*Laughs hysterically.*) What are you talking about?

Strophe   Obsessed.

Phaedra   No.

Strophe   (*Looks at her.*)

Phaedra   Is it that obvious?

Strophe   I'm your daughter.

Phaedra   Do you think he's attractive?

Strophe   I used to.

Phaedra   What changed?

Strophe   I got to know him.

Phaedra   You don't like him?

Strophe   Not particularly.

Phaedra   You don't like Hippolytus?

Strophe   No, not really.

Phaedra   Everyone likes Hippolytus.

Strophe   I live with him.

Phaedra   It's a big house.

Strophe   He's a big man.

Phaedra   You used to spend time together.

Strophe   He wore me out.

Phaedra   You tired of Hippolytus?

Strophe   He bores me.

Phaedra   Bores you?

Strophe   Shitless.

Phaedra   Why? Everyone likes him.

Strophe   I know.

Phaedra   I know what room he's in.

Strophe   He never moves.

Phaedra   Can feel him through the walls. Sense him.
Feel his heartbeat from a mile.

Strophe   Why don't you have an affair, get your mind off
him.

Phaedra   There's a thing between us, an awesome fucking thing, can you feel it? It burns. Meant to be. We were. Meant to be.

Strophe   No.

Phaedra   Brought together.

Strophe   He's twenty years younger than you.

Phaedra   Want to climb inside him work him out.

Strophe   This isn't healthy.

Phaedra   He's not my son.

Strophe   You're married to his father.

Phaedra   He won't come back, too busy being useless.

Strophe   Mother. If someone were to find out.

Phaedra   Can't deny something this big.

Strophe   He's not nice to people when he's slept with them. I've seen him.

Phaedra   Might help me get over him.

Strophe   Treats them like shit.

Phaedra   Can't switch this off. Can't crush it. Can't. Wake up with it, burning me. Think I'll crack open I want him so much. I talk to him. He talks to me, you know, we, we know each other very well, he tells me things, we're very close. About sex and how much it depresses him, and I know –

Strophe   Don't imagine you can cure him.

Phaedra   Know if it was someone who loved you, really loved you –

Strophe   He's poison.

Phaedra   Loved you till it burnt them –

Strophe They do love him. Everyone loves him.
He despises them for it. You'd be no different.

Phaedra You could feel such pleasure.

Strophe Mother. It's me. Strophe, your daughter. Look at
me. Please. Forget this. For my sake.

Phaedra Yours?

Strophe You don't talk about anything else any more.
You don't work. He's all you care about, but you
don't see what he is.

Phaedra I don't talk about him that often.

Strophe No. Most of the time you're with him. Even
when you're not with him you're with him. And
just occasionally, when you remember that you
gave birth to me and not him, you tell me how
ill he is.

Phaedra I'm worried about him.

Strophe You've said. See a doctor.

Phaedra He –

Strophe For yourself, not him.

Phaedra There's nothing wrong with me. I don't know
what to do.

Strophe Stay away from him, go and join Theseus, fuck
someone else, whatever it takes.

Phaedra I can't.

Strophe You can have any man you want.

Phaedra I want him.

Strophe Except him.

Phaedra Any man I want except the man I want.

Strophe Have you ever fucked a man more than once?

Phaedra   This is different.

Strophe   Mother, this family –

Phaedra   Oh I know.

Strophe   If anyone were to find out.

Phaedra   I know, I know.

Strophe   It's the excuse they're all looking for.
We'd be torn apart on the streets.

Phaedra   Yes, yes, no, you're right, yes.

Strophe   Think of Theseus. Why you married him.

Phaedra   I can't remember.

Strophe   Then think of my father.

Phaedra   I know.

Strophe   What would he think?

Phaedra   He'd –

Strophe   Exactly. You can't do it. Can't even think of it.

Phaedra   No.

Strophe   He's a sexual disaster area.

Phaedra   Yes, I –

Strophe   No one must know. No one must know.

Phaedra   You're right, I –

Strophe   No one must know.

Phaedra   No.

Strophe   Not even Hippolytus.

Phaedra   No.

Strophe   What are you going to do?

Phaedra   Get over him.

Scene Four

> **Hippolytus** *is watching television with the sound very low.*
> *He is playing with a remote control car.*
> *It whizzes around the room.*
> *His gaze flits between the car and the television apparently getting pleasure from neither.*
> *He eats from a large bag of assorted sweets on his lap.*
> **Phaedra** *enters carrying a number of wrapped presents.*
> *She stands for a few moments watching him.*
> *He doesn't look at her.*
> **Phaedra** *comes further into the room.*
> *She puts the presents down and begins to tidy the room – she picks up socks and underwear and looks for somewhere to put them. There is nowhere, so she puts them back on the floor in a neat pile.*
> *She picks up the empty crisp and sweet packets and puts them in the bin.*
> **Hippolytus** *watches the television throughout.*
> **Phaedra** *moves to switch on a brighter light.*

Hippolytus   When was the last time you had a fuck?

Phaedra   That's not the sort of question you should ask your stepmother.

Hippolytus   Not Theseus, then. Don't suppose he's keeping it dry either.

Phaedra   I wish you'd call him father.

Hippolytus   Everyone wants a royal cock, I should know.

Phaedra   What are you watching?

Hippolytus   Or a royal cunt if that's your preference.

Phaedra   *(Doesn't respond.)*

Hippolytus   News. Another rape. Child murdered. War somewhere. Few thousand jobs gone. But none of this matters 'cause it's a royal birthday.

Phaedra   Why don't you riot like everyone else?

Hippolytus   I don't care.

Silence.
Hippolytus *plays with his car.*

Hippolytus   Are those for me? Course they're fucking for me.

Phaedra   People brought them to the gate. I think they'd like to have given them to you in person. Taken photos.

Hippolytus   They're poor.

Phaedra   Yes, isn't it charming?

Hippolytus   It's revolting. (*He opens a present.*) What the fuck am I going to do with a bagatelle? What's this? (*He shakes a present.*) Letter bomb. Get rid of this tat, give it to Oxfam, I don't need it.

Phaedra   It's a token of their esteem.

Hippolytus   Less than last year.

Phaedra   Have you had a good birthday?

Hippolytus   Apart from some cunt scratching my motor.

Phaedra   You don't drive.

Hippolytus   Can't now, it's scratched. Token of their contempt.

Silence.
Hippolytus *plays with his car.*

Phaedra   Who gave you that?

Hippolytus   Me. Only way of making sure I get what I want. Wrapped it up and everything.

Silence apart from the TV and car.

Phaedra   What about you?

Hippolytus   What about me? Want a sweet?

Phaedra   I –
No. Thank you.
The last time you –
What you asked me.

Hippolytus   Had a fuck.

Phaedra   Yes.

Hippolytus   Don't know. Last time I went out. When was
that?

Phaedra   Months ago.

Hippolytus   Really? No. Someone came round. Fat bird.
Smelt funny. And I fucked a man in the
garden.

Phaedra   A man?

Hippolytus   Think so. Looked like one but you can never
be sure.

Silence.

Hippolytus   Hate me now?

Phaedra   Course not.

Silence.

Hippolytus   Where's my present, then?

Phaedra   I'm saving it.

Hippolytus   What, for next year?

Phaedra   No. I'll give it to you later.

Hippolytus   When?

Phaedra   Soon.

Hippolytus   Why not now?

Phaedra   Soon. I promise. Soon.

They look at each other in silence.
Hippolytus *looks away.*
He sniffs.
He picks up a sock and examines it.
He smells it.

Phaedra   That's disgusting.

Hippolytus   What is?

Phaedra   Blowing your nose on your sock.

Hippolytus   Only after I've checked I haven't cleaned my
cum up with it first. And I do have them
washed.
Before I wear them.

Silence.
Hippolytus *crashes the car into the wall.*

Hippolytus   What is wrong with you?

Phaedra   What do you mean?

Hippolytus   I was born into this shit, you married it. Was
he a great shag? Fucking must have been.
Every man in the country is sniffing round your
cunt and you pick Theseus, man of the people,
what a wanker.

Phaedra   You only ever talk to me about sex.

Hippolytus   It's my main interest.

Phaedra   I thought you hated it.

Hippolytus   I hate people.

Phaedra   They don't hate you.

Hippolytus   No. They buy me bagatelles.

Phaedra   I meant –

Hippolytus   I know what you meant. You're right.
Women find me much more attractive since

I've become fat. They think I must have a secret.

(*He blows his nose on the sock and discards it.*)

I'm fat. I'm disgusting. I'm miserable. But I get lots of sex. Therefore . . . ?

Phaedra (*Doesn't respond.*)

Hippolytus Come on, Mother, work it out.

Phaedra Don't call me that.

Hippolytus Therefore. I must be very good at it. Yes?

Phaedra (*Doesn't respond.*)

Hippolytus Why shouldn't I call you mother, Mother? I thought that's what was required. One big happy family. The only popular royals ever. Or does it make you feel old?

Phaedra (*Doesn't respond.*)

Hippolytus Hate me now?

Phaedra Why do you want me to hate you?

Hippolytus I don't. But you will. In the end.

Phaedra Never.

Hippolytus They all do.

Phaedra Not me.

They stare at each other.
Hippolytus *looks away.*

Hippolytus Why don't you go and talk to Strophe, she's your child, I'm not. Why all this concern for me?

Phaedra I love you.

Silence.

Hippolytus Why?

Phaedra You're difficult. Moody, cynical, bitter, fat, decadent, spoilt. You stay in bed all day then watch TV all night, you crash around this house with sleep in your eyes and not a thought for anyone. You're in pain. I adore you.

Hippolytus Not very logical.

Phaedra Love isn't.

> **Hippolytus** *and* **Phaedra** *look at each other in silence.*
> *He turns back to the television and car.*

Phaedra Have you ever thought about having sex with me?

Hippolytus I think about having sex with everyone.

Phaedra Would it make you happy?

Hippolytus That's not the word exactly.

Phaedra No, but –
Would you enjoy it?

Hippolytus No. I never do.

Phaedra Then why do it?

Hippolytus Life's too long.

Phaedra I think you'd enjoy it. With me.

Hippolytus Some people do, I suppose. Enjoy that stuff. Have a life.

Phaedra You've got a life.

Hippolytus No. Filling up time. Waiting.

Phaedra For what?

Hippolytus Don't know. Something to happen.

Phaedra This is happening.

Hippolytus   Never does.

Phaedra   Now.

Hippolytus   Till then. Fill it up with tat. Bric-a-brac, bits and bobs, getting by, Christ Almighty wept.

Phaedra   Fill it up with me.

Hippolytus   Some people have it. They're not marking time, they're living. Happy. With a lover. Hate them.

Phaedra   Why?

Hippolytus   Getting dark thank Christ day's nearly over.

A long silence.

Hippolytus   If we fuck we'll never talk again.

Phaedra   I'm not like that.

Hippolytus   I am.

Phaedra   I'm not.

Hippolytus   Course you are.

They stare at each other.

Phaedra   I'm in love with you.

Hippolytus   Why?

Phaedra   You thrill me.

Silence.

Phaedra   Would you like your present now?

Hippolytus   (*Looks at her. Then turns back to the TV.*)

Silence.

Phaedra   I don't know what to do.

Hippolytus   Go away. It's obviously the only thing to do.

They both stare at the television.
Eventually, **Phaedra** *moves over to* **Hippolytus.**
He doesn't look at her.
She undoes his trousers and performs oral sex on him.
He watches the screen throughout and eats his sweets.
As he is about to come he makes a sound.
Phaedra *begins to move her head away – he holds it down and comes in her mouth without taking his eyes off the television.*
He releases her head.
Phaedra *sits up and looks at the television.*
A long silence, broken only by the rustling of **Hippolytus'** *sweet bag.*
Phaedra *cries.*

Hippolytus   There. Mystery over.

Silence.

Phaedra   Will you get jealous?

Hippolytus   Of what?

Phaedra   When your father comes back.

Hippolytus   What's it got to do with me?

Phaedra   I've never been unfaithful before.

Hippolytus   That much was obvious.

Phaedra   I'm sorry.

Hippolytus   I've had worse.

Phaedra   I did it because I'm in love with you.

Hippolytus   Don't be. I don't like it.

Phaedra   I want this to happen again.

Hippolytus   No you don't.

Phaedra   I do.

Hippolytus   What for?

Phaedra   Pleasure?

Hippolytus You enjoyed that?

Phaedra I want to be with you.

Hippolytus But did you enjoy it?

Phaedra (*Doesn't respond.*)

Hippolytus No. You hate it as much as me if only you'd admit it.

Phaedra I wanted to see your face when you came.

Hippolytus Why?

Phaedra I'd like to see you lose yourself.

Hippolytus It's not a pleasant sight.

Phaedra Why, what do you look like?

Hippolytus Every other stupid fucker.

Phaedra I love you.

Hippolytus No.

Phaedra So much.

Hippolytus Don't even know me.

Phaedra I want you to make me come.

Hippolytus Can't stand post-coital chats.
There's never anything to say.

Phaedra I want you –

Hippolytus This isn't about me.

Phaedra I do.

Hippolytus Fuck someone else imagine it's me. Shouldn't be difficult, everyone looks the same when they come.

Phaedra Not when they burn you.

Hippolytus No one burns me.

Phaedra   What about that woman?

Silence.
Hippolytus *looks at her.*

Hippolytus   What?

Phaedra   Lena, weren't you –

Hippolytus   (*Grabs* **Phaedra** *by the throat.*)

> Don't ever mention her again.
> Don't say her name to me, don't refer to
> her, don't even think about her, understand?
> Understand?

Phaedra   (*Nods.*)

Hippolytus   No one burns me, no one fucking touches me.
So don't try.

He releases her.
Silence.

Phaedra   Why do you have sex if you hate it so much?

Hippolytus   I'm bored.

Phaedra   I thought you were supposed to be good at it.
Is everyone this disappointed?

Hippolytus   Not when I try.

Phaedra   When do you try?

Hippolytus   Don't any more.

Phaedra   Why not?

Hippolytus   It's boring.

Phaedra   You're just like your father.

Hippolytus   That's what your daughter said.

A beat, then **Phaedra** *slaps him around the face as hard as
she can.*

Hippolytus   She's less passionate but more practised. I go for technique every time.

Phaedra   Did you make her come?

Hippolytus   Yes.

Phaedra   (*Opens her mouth to speak. She can't.*)

Hippolytus   It's dead now. Face it. Can't happen again.

Phaedra   Why not?

Hippolytus   Wouldn't be about me. Never was.

Phaedra   You can't stop me loving you.

Hippolytus   Can.

Phaedra   No. You're alive.

Hippolytus   Wake up.

Phaedra   You burn me.

Hippolytus   Now you've had me, fuck someone else.

Silence.

Phaedra   Will I see you again?

Hippolytus   You know where I am.

Silence.

Hippolytus   Do I get my present now?

Phaedra   (*Opens her mouth but is momentarily lost for words. Then.*)

You're a heartless bastard.

Hippolytus   Exactly.

Phaedra *begins to leave.*

Hippolytus   Phaedra.

Phaedra   (*Looks at him.*)

Hippolytus   See a doctor. I've got gonorrhoea.

Phaedra   (*Opens her mouth. No sound comes out.*)

Hippolytus   Hate me now?

Phaedra   (*Tries to speak. A long silence. Eventually.*)

No. Why do you hate me?

Hippolytus   Because you hate yourself.

Phaedra *leaves.*

Scene Five

Hippolytus *is standing in front of a mirror with his tongue out.*
Strophe *enters.*

Strophe   Hide.

Hippolytus   Green tongue.

Strophe   Hide, idiot.

Hippolytus *turns to her and shows her his tongue.*

Hippolytus   Fucking moss. Inch of pleurococcus on my
tongue. Looks like the top of a wall.

Strophe   Hippolytus.

Hippolytus   Showed it to a bloke in the bogs, still wanted to
shag me.

Strophe   Have you looked out the window?

Hippolytus   Major halitosis.

Strophe   Look.

Hippolytus   Haven't seen you for ages, how are you?

Strophe   Burning.

Hippolytus   You'd never know we live in the same
house.

Strophe For fuck's sake, hide.

Hippolytus Why, what have I done?

Strophe My mother's accusing you of rape.

Hippolytus She is? How exciting.

Strophe This isn't a joke.

Hippolytus I'm sure.

Strophe Did you do it?

Hippolytus What?

Strophe Did you rape her?

Hippolytus I don't know. What does that mean?

Strophe Did you have sex with her?

Hippolytus Ah. Got you.
Does it matter?

Strophe Does it *matter*?

Hippolytus Does it matter.

Strophe Yes.

Hippolytus Why?

Strophe *Why*?

Hippolytus Yes, why, I do wish you wouldn't repeat
everything I say, why?

Strophe She's my mother.

Hippolytus So?

Strophe My mother says she was raped.
She says you raped her.
I want to know if you had sex with my mother.

Hippolytus Because she's your mother or because of what
people will say?

Strophe   Because she's my mother.

Hippolytus   Because you still want me or because you want to know if she was better than you?

Strophe   Because she's my mother.

Hippolytus   Because she's your mother.

Strophe   Did you have sex with her?

Hippolytus   I don't think so.

Strophe   Was there any sexual contact between you and my mother?

Hippolytus   Sexual contact?

Strophe   You know exactly what I mean.

Hippolytus   Don't get stroppy, Strophe.

Strophe   Did she want to do it?

Hippolytus   You should have been a lawyer.

Strophe   Did you make her?

Hippolytus   You're wasted as a pseudo-princess.

Strophe   Did you force her?

Hippolytus   Did I force you?

Strophe   There aren't words for what you did to me.

Hippolytus   Then perhaps rape is the best she can do. Me. A rapist. Things are looking up.

Strophe   Hippolytus.

Hippolytus   At the very least it's not boring.

Strophe   You'll be lynched for this.

Hippolytus   Do you think?

Strophe   If you did it I'll help them.

Hippolytus   Of course. Not my sister after all. One of my victims.

Strophe   If you didn't I'll stand by you.

Hippolytus   A rapist?

Strophe   Burn with you.

Hippolytus   Why?

Strophe   Sake of the family.

Hippolytus   Ah.

Strophe   You're my brother.

Hippolytus   No I'm not.

Strophe   To me.

Hippolytus   Strange. The one person in this family who has no claim to its history is the most sickeningly loyal. Poor relation who wants to be what she never will.

Strophe   I'll die for this family.

Hippolytus   Yes. You probably will.
I told her about us.

Strophe   You what?

Hippolytus   Yes. And I mentioned that you'd had her husband.

Strophe   No.

Hippolytus   I didn't say you fucked him on their wedding night, but since he left the day after –

Strophe   Mother.

Hippolytus   A rapist. Better than a fat boy who fucks.

Strophe   You're smiling.

Hippolytus   I am.

Strophe   You're a heartless bastard, you know that?

Hippolytus   It's been said.

Strophe   This is your fault.

Hippolytus   Of course.

Strophe   She was my mother, Hippolytus, my mother.
What did you do to her?

Hippolytus   (*Looks at her.*)

Strophe   She's dead you fucking bastard.

Hippolytus   Don't be stupid.

Strophe   Yes.
What did you do to her, what did you fucking do?

Strophe *batters him about the head.*
Hippolytus *catches her arms and holds her so she can't hit him.*
Strophe *sobs, then breaks down and cries, then wails
uncontrollably.*

Strophe   What have I done? What have I done?

Hippolytus' *hold turns into an embrace.*

Hippolytus   Wasn't you, Strophe, you're not to blame.

Strophe   Never even told her I loved her.

Hippolytus   She knew.

Strophe   No.

Hippolytus   She was your mother.

Strophe   She –

Hippolytus   She knew, she knew, she loved you.
Nothing to blame yourself for.

Strophe   You told her about us.

Hippolytus   Then blame me.

Strophe   You told her about Theseus.

Hippolytus   Yes. Blame me.

Strophe   You –

Hippolytus   Me. Blame me.

A long silence.
Hippolytus *and* **Strophe** *hold each other.*

Hippolytus   What happened?

Strophe   Hung.

Silence.

Strophe   Note saying you'd raped her.

A long silence.

Hippolytus   She shouldn't have taken it so seriously.

Strophe   She loved you.

Hippolytus   (*Looks at her.*) Did she?

Strophe   Tell me you didn't rape her.

Hippolytus   Love me?

Strophe   Tell me you didn't do it.

Hippolytus   She says I did and she's dead. Believe her. Easier all round.

Strophe   What is wrong with you?

Hippolytus   This is her present to me.

Strophe   What?

Hippolytus   Not many people get a chance like this. This isn't tat. This isn't bric-a-brac.

Strophe   Deny it. There's a riot.

Hippolytus   Life at last.

Strophe   Burning down the palace. You have to deny it.

Hippolytus   Are you insane? She died doing this for me. I'm doomed.

Strophe   Deny it.

Hippolytus   Absolutely fucking doomed.

Strophe   For me. Deny it.

Hippolytus   No.

Strophe   You're not a rapist. I can't believe that.

Hippolytus   Me neither.

Strophe   Please.

Hippolytus   Fucked. Finished.

Strophe   I'll help you hide.

Hippolytus   She really did love me.

Strophe   You didn't do it.

Hippolytus   Bless her.

Strophe   Did you?

Hippolytus   No. I didn't.

He begins to leave.

Strophe   Where are you going?

Hippolytus   I'm turning myself in.

He leaves.
Strophe *sits alone for a few moments, thinking.*
She gets up and follows him.

Scene Six

A prison cell.

Hippolytus *sits alone.*
A **Priest** *enters.*

Priest My son.

Hippolytus Bit of a come down. Always suspected the world didn't smell of fresh paint and flowers.

Priest I may be able to help you.

Hippolytus Smells of piss and human sweat. Most unpleasant.

Priest Son.

Hippolytus You're not my father. He won't be visiting.

Priest Is there anything you need?

Hippolytus Got a single cell.

Priest I can help you.

Hippolytus Don't need tat.

Priest Spiritually.

Hippolytus Beyond that.

Priest No one is beyond redemption.

Hippolytus Nothing to confess.

Priest Your sister told us.

Hippolytus Us?

Priest She explained the situation to me.

Hippolytus She's not my sister.
Admit, yes. Confess, no.
I admit it. The rape. I did it.

Priest Do you feel remorse?

Hippolytus Will you be giving evidence?

Priest That depends.

Hippolytus No. No remorse. Joy, in fact.

Priest At your mother's death?

Hippolytus   Suicide, not death. She wasn't my mother.

Priest   You feel joy at your stepmother's suicide?

Hippolytus   No. She was human.

Priest   So where do you find your joy?

Hippolytus   Within.

Priest   I find that hard to believe.

Hippolytus   Course you do. You think life has no
meaning unless we have another person in it
to torture us.

Priest   I have no one to torture me.

Hippolytus   You have the worst lover of all. Not only
does he think he's perfect, he is. I'm satisfied
to be alone.

Priest   Self-satisfaction is a contradiction in terms.

Hippolytus   I can rely on me. I never let me down.

Priest   True satisfaction comes from love.

Hippolytus   What when love dies? Alarm clock rings it's
time to wake up, what then?

Priest   Love never dies. It evolves.

Hippolytus   You're dangerous.

Priest   Into respect. Consideration.
Have you considered your family?

Hippolytus   What about it?

Priest   It's not an ordinary family.

Hippolytus   No. None of us are related to each other.

Priest   Royalty is chosen. Because you are more privileged
than most you are also more culpable. God –

Hippolytus There is no God. There is. No God.

Priest Perhaps you'll find there is. And what will you do then? There's no repentance in the next life, only in this one.

Hippolytus What do you suggest, a last minute conversion just in case? Die as if there is a God, knowing that there isn't? No. If there is a God, I'd like to look him in the face knowing I'd died as I'd lived. In conscious sin.

Priest Hippolytus.

Hippolytus I'm sure God would be intelligent enough to see through any eleventh hour confession of mine.

Priest Do you know what the unforgivable sin is?

Hippolytus Of course.

Priest You are in danger of committing it. It's not just your soul at stake, it's the future of your family –

Hippolytus Ah.

Priest Your country.

Hippolytus Why do I always forget this?

Priest Your sexual indiscretions are of no interest to anyone. But the stability of the nation's morals is. You are a guardian of those morals. You will answer to God for the collapse of the country you and your family lead.

Hippolytus I'm not responsible.

Priest Then deny the rape. And confess that sin. Now.

Hippolytus Before I've committed it?

Priest Too late after.

Hippolytus   Yes. The nature of the sin precludes
confession.
I couldn't confess if I wanted to.
I don't want to. That's the sin. Correct?

Priest   It's not too late.

Hippolytus   Correct.

Priest   God is merciful. He chose you.

Hippolytus   Bad choice.

Priest   Pray with me. Save yourself. And your country.
Don't commit that sin.

Hippolytus   What bothers you more, the destruction of
my soul or the end of my family? I'm not in
danger of committing the unforgivable sin. I
already have.

Priest   Don't say it.

Hippolytus   Fuck God. Fuck the monarchy.

Priest   Lord, look down on this man you chose, forgive his
sin which comes from the intelligence you blessed
him with.

Hippolytus   I can't sin against a God I don't believe in.

A long silence.

Priest   No.

Hippolytus   A non-existent God can't forgive.

Priest   No. You must forgive yourself.

Hippolytus   I've lived by honesty let me die by it.

Priest   If truth is your absolute you will die.
If life is your absolute –

Hippolytus   I've chosen my path. I'm fucking doomed.

Priest   No.

Hippolytus   Let me die.

Priest   No. Forgive yourself.

Hippolytus   (*Thinks hard.*)

I can't.

Priest   Why not?

Hippolytus   Do you believe in God?

Priest   (*Looks at him.*)

Hippolytus   I know what I am. And always will be. But you.
You sin knowing you'll confess. Then you're
forgiven. And then you start all over again.
How do you dare mock a God so powerful?
Unless you don't really believe.

Priest   This is your confession, not mine.

Hippolytus   Then why are you on your knees? God
certainly is merciful. If I were him I'd
despise you. I'd wipe you off the face of the
earth for your dishonesty.

Priest   You're not God.

Hippolytus   No. A prince. God on earth. But not God.
Fortunate for all concerned. I'd not allow
you to sin knowing you'd confess and get
away with it.

Priest   Heaven would be empty.

Hippolytus   A kingdom of honest men, honestly sinning.
And death for those who try to cover
their arse.

Priest   What do you think forgiveness is?

Hippolytus   It may be enough for you, but I have no
intention of covering my arse. I killed a
woman and I will be punished for it by

hypocrites who I shall take down with me.
May we burn in hell. God may be all powerful,
but there's one thing he can't do.

Priest   There is a kind of purity in you.

Hippolytus   He can't make me good.

Priest   No.

Hippolytus   Last line of defence for the honest man.
Free will is what distinguishes us from the
animals.

(*He undoes his trousers.*)

And I have no intention of behaving like a
fucking animal.

Priest   (*Performs oral sex on* **Hippolytus.**)

Hippolytus   Leave that to you.

(*He comes.*
He rests his hand on top of the **Priest***'s head.*)

Go.
Confess.
Before you burn.

Scene Seven

Phaedra*'s body lies on a funeral pyre, covered.*
Theseus *enters.*
He approaches the pyre.
He lifts the cover and looks at **Phaedra***'s face.*
He lets the cover drop.
He kneels by **Phaedra***'s body.*
*He tears at his clothes, then skin, then hair, more and more
frantically until he is exhausted.*
But he does not cry.
He stands and lights the funeral pyre – **Phaedra** *goes up in
flames.*

Theseus   I'll kill him.

Scene Eight

Outside the court.

A crowd of men, women and children has gathered, including **Theseus** *and* **Strophe**, *both disguised.*

Theseus   Come far?

Man 1   Newcastle.

Woman 1   Brought the kids.

Child   And a barby. [barbecue]

Man 1   String him up, they should.

Woman 2   The bastard.

Man 1   Whole fucking pack of them.

Woman 1   Set an example.

Man 1   What do they take us for?

Woman 1   Parasites.

Man 2   We pay the raping bastard.

Man 1   No more.

Man 2   They're nothing special.

Woman 1   Raped his own mother.

Woman 2   The bastard.

Man 2   She was the only one had anything going for her.

Theseus   He'll walk.

Man 2   I'll be waiting at the fucking gate.

Man 1   Won't be the only one.

Woman 1   He's admitted it.

Strophe   That means nothing.

Woman 2   The bastard.

Theseus   Might go in his favour. Sorry your honour, reading my Bible every day, never do it again, case dismissed. Not going to lock a prince up, are they? Whatever he's done.

Man 2   That's right.

Man 1   No justice.

Theseus   Member of the royal family. Crown against the crown? They're not stupid.

Man 1   Pig-shit thick, the lot of them.

Man 2   She was all right.

Man 1   She's dead.

Theseus   You don't hang on to the crown for centuries without something between your ears.

Man 2   That's right.

Theseus   Show trial. Him in the dock, sacrifice the reputation of a minor prince, expel him from the family.

Man 2   Exactly, exactly.

Theseus   Say they've rid themselves of the corrupting element. But the monarchy remains intact.

Man 1   What shall we do?

Man 2   Justice for all.

Woman 1   He must die.

Man 2   Has to die.

Man 1   For our sake.

Man 2   And hers.

Woman 1 Don't deserve to live. I've got kids.

Man 1 We've all got kids.

Woman 1 You got kids?

Theseus Not any more.

Woman 2 Poor bastard.

Man 2 Knows what we're talking about then, don't he.

Man 1 Scum should die.

Woman 1 Here he comes.

Woman 2 The bastard.

> As **Hippolytus** *is taken past, the crowd scream abuse and hurl rocks.*

Woman 2 Bastard!

Man 1 Die, scum!

Woman 1 Rot in hell, bastard!

Man 2 Royal raping bastard!

> **Hippolytus** *breaks free from the* **Policemen** *holding him and hurls himself into the crowd.*
> *He falls into the arms of* **Theseus**.

Man 1 Kill him. Kill the royal slag.

> **Hippolytus** *looks into* **Theseus**' *face.*

Hippolytus You.

> **Theseus** *hesitates, then kisses him full on the lips and pushes him into the arms of* **Man 2**.

Theseus Kill him.

> **Man 2** *holds* **Hippolytus**.
> **Man 1** *takes a tie from around a child's neck and puts it around* **Hippolytus**' *throat. He strangles* **Hippolytus**, *who is kicked by*

the **Women** *as he chokes into semi-consciousness.*
Woman 2 *produces a knife.*

Strophe   No! No! Don't hurt him, don't kill him!

Man 2   Listen to her.

Man 1   Defending an in-bred.

Woman 1   What sort of a woman are you?

Theseus   Defending a rapist.

> **Theseus** *pulls* **Strophe** *away from* **Woman 2** *who she is*
> *attacking.*
> *He rapes her.*
> *The crowd watch and cheer.*
> *When* **Theseus** *has finished he cuts her throat.*

Strophe   Theseus.
               Hippolytus.
               Innocent.
               Mother.
               Oh, Mother.

She dies.
Man 1 *pulls down* **Hippolytus'** *trousers.*
Woman 2 *cuts off his genitals.*
They are thrown onto the barbecue.
The children cheer.
A child takes them off the barbecue and throws them at another
child, who screams and runs away.
Much laughter.
Someone retrieves them and they are thrown to a dog.
Theseus *takes the knife.*
He cuts **Hippolytus** *from groin to chest.*
Hippolytus' *bowels are torn out and thrown onto the barbecue.*
He is kicked and stoned and spat on.
Hippolytus *looks at the body of* **Strophe**.

Hippolytus   Strophe.

Theseus   Strophe.

Theseus *looks closely at the woman he has raped and murdered.*
He recognises her with horror.
When **Hippolytus** *is completely motionless, the police who have*
been watching wade into the crowd, hitting them randomly.
The crowd disperses with the exception of **Theseus**.
Two **Policemen** *stand looking down at* **Hippolytus**.

Policeman 1   Poor bastard.

Policeman 2   You joking?

    (*He kicks* **Hippolytus** *hard.*)

    I've got two daughters.

Policeman 1   Should move him.

Policeman 2   Let him rot.

  Policeman 2 *spits on* **Hippolytus.**
  They leave.
  Hippolytus *is motionless.*
  Theseus *is sitting by* **Strophe**'*s body.*

Theseus   Hippolytus.
    Son.
    I never liked you.

    (*To* **Strophe**.)

    I'm sorry.
    Didn't know it was you.
    God forgive me I didn't know.
    If I'd known it was you I'd never have –

    (*To* **Hippolytus**.)

    You hear me, I didn't know.

  Theseus *cuts his own throat and bleeds to death.*
  The three bodies lie completely still.
  Eventually, **Hippolytus** *opens his eyes and looks at the sky.*

Hippolytus   Vultures.

    (*He manages a smile.*)

If there could have been more moments
like this.

Hippolytus *dies.*
A vulture descends and begins to eat his body.

Cleansed

My thanks to all the writers, directors and actors, both at New Dramatists and in the UK, who gave their time to help develop this play.

For the patients and staff of ES3.

Cleansed was first performed at the Royal Court Theatre Downstairs on 30 April 1998. The cast was as follows:

Graham	Martin Marquez
Tinker	Stuart McQuarrie
Carl	James Cunningham
Rod	Danny Cerqueira
Grace	Suzan Sylvester
Robin	Daniel Evans
Woman	Victoria Harwood

Director	James Macdonald
Designer	Jeremy Herbert
Lighting Designer	Nigel Edwards
Sound Designer	Paul Arditti
Movement	Wayne MacGregor

Author's note

A stroke (/) indicates the point of interruption in overlapping dialogue.

Stage directions in brackets function as lines.

Where punctuation is missing, it is to indicate delivery.

Editor's note

This edition of *Cleansed*, first reprinted in 2000, incorporates minor revisions made to the original text by Sarah Kane shortly before her death. It should therefore be regarded as the definitive version in all respects.

Scene One

Just inside the perimeter fence of a university.
It is snowing.

Tinker *is heating smack on a silver spoon.*
Graham *enters.*

Graham Tinker.

Tinker I'm cooking.

Graham I want out.

Tinker (*Looks up.*)

Silence.

Tinker No.

Graham Is that for me?

Tinker I don't use.

Graham More.

Tinker No.

Graham It's not enough.

Tinker I'm a dealer not a doctor.

Graham Are you my friend?

Tinker I don't think so.

Graham Then what difference will it make?

Tinker It won't end here.

Graham My sister, she wants –

Tinker Don't tell me.

Graham I know my limits. Please.

Tinker You know what will happen to me?

Graham Yes.

Tinker It's just the beginning.

Graham Yes.

Tinker You'll leave me to that?

Graham We're not friends.

Pause.

Tinker No.

Graham No regrets.

Tinker (*Thinks. Then adds another large lump of smack to the spoon.*)

Graham More.

Tinker (*Looks at him. Then puts on another lump. He adds lemon juice and heats the smack. He fills the syringe.*)

Graham (*Searches for a vein with difficulty.*)

Tinker (*Injects into the corner of* **Graham***'s eye.*)

Count backwards from ten.

Graham Ten. Nine. Eight.

Tinker Your legs are heavy.

Graham Seven. Six. Five.

Tinker Your head is light.

Graham Four. Four. Five.

Tinker Life is sweet.

Graham This is what it's like.

They look at each other.

Graham (*Smiles.*)

Tinker (*Looks away.*)

Graham Thank you, Doctor.

(*He slumps.*)

Tinker   Graham?

Silence.

Tinker   Four.
Three.
Two.
One.
Zero.

Scene Two

Rod *and* **Carl** *sit on the college green just inside the perimeter fence of the university.*

Midsummer – the sun is shining.
The sound of a cricket match in progress on the other side of the fence.

Carl *takes off his ring.*

Carl   Can I have your ring?

Rod   I'm not going to be your husband, Carl.

Carl   How do you know?

Rod   I'm not going to be anyone's husband.

Carl   I want you to have my ring.

Rod   What for?

Carl   A sign.

Rod   Of what?

Carl   Commitment.

Rod   You've known me three months. It's suicide.

Carl   Please.

Rod   You'd die for me?

Carl   Yes.

Rod (*Holds out his hand.*) I don't like this.

Carl (*Closes his eyes and puts the ring on* **Rod***'s finger.*)

Rod What are you thinking?

Carl That I'll always love you.

Rod (*Laughs.*)

Carl That I'll never betray you.

Rod (*Laughs more.*)

Carl That I'll never lie to you.

Rod You just have.

Carl Baby –

Rod Sweetheart honey baby I have a name. You love me so much why can't you remember my name?

Carl Rod.

Rod Rod. Rod.

Carl Can I have your ring?

Rod No.

Carl Why not?

Rod I wouldn't die for you.

Carl That's all right.

Rod I can't promise you anything.

Carl I don't mind.

Rod I do.

Carl Please.

Rod (*Takes off his ring and hands it to* **Carl**.)

Carl Will you put it on my finger?

Rod No.

Carl   Please.

Rod   No.

Carl   I don't expect anything.

Rod   Yes you do.

Carl   You don't have to say anything.

Rod   I do.

Carl   Please, Baby.

Rod   Fuck's/sake –

Carl   Rod, Rod, sorry. Please.

Rod   (*Takes the ring and* **Carl***'s hand.*)

   Listen. I'm saying this once.

   (*He puts the ring on* **Carl***'s finger.*)

   I love you *now*.
   I'm with you *now*.
   I'll do my best, moment to moment, not to betray
   you.
   Now.
   That's it. No more. Don't make me lie to you.

Carl   I'm not lying to you.

Rod   Grow up.

Carl   I'll never turn away from you.

Rod   Carl. Anyone you can think of, someone somewhere
   got bored with fucking them.

Carl   Why are you so cynical?

Rod   I'm old.

Carl   You're thirty-four.

Rod   Thirty-nine. I lied.

Carl   Still.

Rod   Don't trust me.

Pause.

Carl   I do.

They kiss.
Tinker *is watching.*

Scene Three

The White Room – the university sanatorium.

Grace *stands alone, waiting.*
Tinker *enters consulting a file.*

Tinker   He's been dead six months. We don't normally keep the clothes that long.

Grace   What happens to them?

Tinker   Recycled. Or incinerated.

Grace   Recycled?

Tinker   Most likely incinerated, but –

Grace   You give them to someone else?

Tinker   Yes.

Grace   Isn't that very unhygienic?

Tinker   He died of an overdose.

Grace   Then why burn his body?

Tinker   He was an addict.

Grace   You thought nobody cared.

Tinker   I wasn't here at the time.

Grace   I need to see his clothes.

Tinker   I'm sorry.

Grace   You gave my brother's clothes to someone else, I won't leave until I've seen them.

Tinker   (*Doesn't respond.*)

Grace   What does it matter to you? Give me his clothes.

Tinker   I'm not allowed to let anything leave the grounds.

Grace   I just need to see them.

Tinker   (*Considers. Then goes to the door and calls.*)

Robin!

They wait. A nineteen year old boy enters.

Tinker   There.

Grace   (*To* **Robin**.) Take off your clothes.

Robin   Miss?

Grace   Grace.

Tinker   Do it.

Robin   (*Takes off his clothes, down to his underpants.*)

Grace   All of them.

Robin   (*Looks at* **Tinker**.)

Tinker   (*Considers, then nods.*)

Robin *removes his underpants and stands shivering with his hands over his genitals.*
Grace *undresses completely.*
Robin *watches, terrified.*
Tinker *looks at the floor.*
Grace *dresses in* **Robin**'s/**Graham**'s *clothes.*
When fully dressed, she stands for a few moments, completely still.
She begins to shake.
She breaks down and wails uncontrollably.
She collapses.
Tinker *lifts her onto a bed.*
She lashes out – he handcuffs both arms to the bed rails.
He injects her. She relaxes.
Tinker *strokes her hair.*

Grace I'm not leaving.

Tinker You are. You won't find him here.

Grace I want to stay.

Tinker It's not right.

Grace I'm staying.

Tinker You'll be moved.

Grace I look like him. Say you thought I was a man.

Tinker I can't protect you.

Grace I don't want you to.

Tinker You shouldn't be here. You're not well.

Grace Treat me as a patient.

Tinker (*Considers in silence. Then takes a bottle of pills from his pocket.*)

Show me your tongue.

Grace (*Sticks out her tongue.*)

Tinker (*Puts a pill on her tongue.*)

Swallow.

Grace (*Does.*)

Tinker I'm not responsible, Grace.

He leaves.
Grace *and* **Robin** *stare at each other,* **Robin** *still naked, hands covering his genitals.*

Grace Dress.

Robin (*Looks at* **Grace***'s clothes on the floor.*
He puts them on.)

Grace Write for me.

Robin   (*Blinks.*)

Grace   I need you to tell my father I'm staying here.

    Pause.

Robin   Leaving soon. Going to my mum's.

Grace   (*Stares.*)

Robin   If I don't mess up again.
Going to my mum's, get myself sorted so I –
Get sorted.

Grace   (*Stares.*)

Robin   What you doing here, don't have girls here.
Staring at me.

Grace   Write for me. (*She rattles her handcuffs.*)

Robin   Voice told me to kill myself.

Grace   (*Stares.*)

Robin   Safe now. Nobody kills themself here.

Grace   (*Stares.*)

Robin   Nobody wants to die.

Grace   (*Stares.*)

Robin   I don't want to die do you want to die?

Grace   (*Stares.*)

Robin   Could be pretty soon, me leaving.
Could be in thirty, Tinker said.
Could be –

Grace   You can't write, can you.

Robin   (*Opens his mouth to answer but can't think of anything to say.*)

Grace   It's not the end of the world.

Robin   (*Tries to speak. Nothing.*)

Scene Four

The Red Room – the university sports hall.

Carl *is being heavily beaten by an unseen group of men.*
We hear the sound of the blows and **Carl***'s body reacts as if he has received the blow.*
Tinker *holds up his arm and the beating stops.*
He drops his arm. The beating resumes.

Carl   Please. Doctor. Please.

Tinker *holds up his arm. The beating stops.*

Tinker   Yes?

Carl   I can't –
Any more.

Tinker *drops his arm.*
The beating continues methodically until **Carl** *is unconscious.*
Tinker *holds up his arm. The beating stops.*

Tinker   Don't kill him.
Save him.

(*He kisses* **Carl***'s face gently.*)

Carl   (*Opens his eyes.*)

Tinker   There's a vertical passage through your body, a straight line through which an object can pass without immediately killing you. Starts here.

(*He touches* **Carl***'s anus.*)

Carl   (*Stiffens with fear.*)

Tinker   Can take a pole, push it up here, avoiding all major organs, until it emerges here.

(*He touches* **Carl***'s right shoulder.*)

Die eventually of course. From starvation if nothing else gets you first.

Carl's *trousers are pulled down and a pole is pushed a few inches up his anus.*

Carl   Christ no

Tinker   What's your boyfriend's name?

Carl   Jesus

Tinker   Can you describe his genitals?

Carl   No

Tinker   When was the last time you sucked his cock?

Carl   I

Tinker   Do you take it up the arse?

Carl   Please

Tinker   Don't give it, I can see that.

Carl   No

Tinker   Close your eyes imagine it's him.

Carl   Please God no I

Tinker   Rodney Rodney split me in half.

Carl   Please don't fucking kill me God

Tinker   I love you Rod I'd die for you.

Carl   Not me   please not me   don't kill me   Rod not me   don't kill me   ROD NOT ME   ROD NOT ME

The pole is removed.
Rod *falls from a great height and lands next to* **Carl**.
Silence.

Tinker   I'm not going to kill either of you.

Carl   I couldn't help it, Rod, was out my mouth before I –

Tinker   Shh shh shh.
No regrets.

(*He strokes* **Carl**'s *hair.*)

Show me your tongue.

Carl *sticks out his tongue.*
Tinker *produces a large pair of scissors and cuts off* **Carl***'s tongue.*
Carl *waves his arms, his mouth open, full of blood, no sound emerging.*
Tinker *takes the ring from* **Rod***'s finger and puts it in* **Carl***'s mouth.*

Tinker   Swallow.

Carl   (*Swallows the ring.*)

Scene Five

The White Room.

Grace *is lying in bed.*
She wakes and stares at the ceiling.
She takes her hands from under the sheet and looks at them – they are free.
She rubs her wrists.
She sits up.
Graham *is sitting at the end of her bed.*
He smiles at her.

Graham   Hello, Sunshine.

Silence.
Grace *stares at him.*
She smacks him around the face as hard as she can, then hugs him to her as tightly as possible.
She holds his face in her hands and looks closely at him.

Grace   You're clean.

Graham   (*Smiles.*)

Grace   Don't ever leave me again.

Graham   No.

Grace   Swear.

Graham   On my life.

Pause. They look at each other in silence.

Graham   More like me than I ever was.

Grace   Teach me.

> **Graham** *dances – a dance of love for* **Grace**.
> **Grace** *dances opposite him, copying his movements.*
> *Gradually, she takes on the masculinity of his movement, his facial expression. Finally, she no longer has to watch him – she mirrors him perfectly as they dance exactly in time.*
> *When she speaks, her voice is more like his.*

Graham   You're good at this.

Grace   Good at this.

Graham   Very good.

Grace   Very good.

Graham   So / very very good.

Grace   Very very good.

Graham   (*Stops and considers her.*)

> I never knew myself, Grace.

Grace   (*Stops mirroring him, confused.*)

> You've always been an angel.

Graham   No. I just look good.

> (*He smiles at her confusion and takes her in his arms.*)

> Not so serious. You're gorgeous when you smile.

They begin to dance slowly, very close together.
They sing the first verse of 'You Are My Sunshine' by Jim Davis and Charles Mitchell.
Their voices trail off and they stand staring at each other.

Grace   They burned your body.

Graham   I'm here. I went away but now I'm back and
nothing else matters.

They stare at each other.
She touches his face.

Grace   If I –

(*She touches his lips.*)

Put my –

(*She puts her finger in his mouth.*)

They stare at each other, terrified.
She kisses him very gently on the lips.

Grace   Love me or kill me, Graham.

He hesitates.
Then kisses her, slowly and gently at first, then harder and deeper.

Graham   I used to . . . think about you and . . .
I used to . . . wish it was you when I . . .
Used to . . .

Grace   Doesn't matter. You went away but now you're
back and nothing else matters.

Graham *takes off her shirt and stares at her breasts.*

Graham   Makes no difference now.

He sucks her right breast.
She undoes his trousers and touches his penis.
They take off the rest of their clothes, watching each other.
They stand naked and look at each other's bodies.
They slowly embrace.
They begin to make love, slowly at first, then hard, fast, urgent,
finding each other's rhythm is the same as their own.
They come together.
They hold each other, him inside her, not moving.
A sunflower bursts through the floor and grows above their heads.
When it is fully grown, **Graham** *pulls it towards him and*
smells it.

He smiles.

Graham   Lovely.

Scene Six

*The Black Room – the showers in the university sports hall
converted into peep-show booths.*

Tinker *enters.*
He sits in a booth.
He takes off his jacket and lays it over his lap.
He undoes his trousers and puts his hand inside.
With his other hand he puts a token in the slot.
The flap opens and he looks in.
A **Woman** *is dancing.*
Tinker *watches for a while, masturbating.*
He stops and looks at the floor.

Tinker   Don't dance, I –
          Can I see your face?

The **Woman** *stops dancing and considers.*
After a moment she sits.

Tinker   *(Doesn't look at her.)*

Woman   *(Waits.)*

Tinker   What you doing here?

Woman   I like it.

Tinker   It's not right.

Woman   I know.

Tinker   Can we be friends?

The flap closes.
Tinker *puts in two more tokens.*
The flap opens.
The **Woman** *is dancing.*

Tinker   Don't, I –
          Your face.

Woman   (*Sits.*)

Tinker   (*Doesn't look at her.*)

            What you doing here?

Woman   I don't know.

Tinker   You shouldn't be here. It's not right.

Woman   I know.

Tinker   I can help.

Woman   How?

Tinker   I'm a doctor.

Woman   (*Doesn't respond.*)

Tinker   You know what that means?

Woman   Yes.

Tinker   Can we be friends?

Woman   I don't think so.

Tinker   No, but –

Woman   No.

Tinker   I'll be anything you need.

Woman   Can't.

Tinker   Yes.

Woman   Too late.

Tinker   Let me try.

Woman   No.

Tinker   Please. I won't let you down.

Woman   (*Laughs.*)

Tinker   Trust me.

Woman   Why?

Tinker   I won't turn away from you.

Woman   Won't face me either.

Tinker   I'll give you whatever you want, Grace.

Woman   (*Doesn't answer.*)

Tinker   (*Looks at her face for the first time.*)

I promise.

The flap closes.
Tinker *has no more tokens.*

Scene Seven

The Round Room – the university library.

Grace *and* **Robin** *sit together looking at a piece of paper. Both still wear each other's clothes.*
Robin *holds a pencil.*
Graham *is watching.*

Grace   It's talking without your voice. Same words you use all the time. Each letter corresponds to a sound. If you can remember which sound corresponds to which letter you can start building words.

Robin   That letter don't look like it sounds.

Grace   R.

Robin   That one does/but that one don't.

Grace   O. You know what this word/says?

Robin   Robin, I know it's my name because you told/me.

Grace   All right, I want you to write a word –

Robin   Grace.

Grace   My name, so you think it looks like it sounds.

Robin   (*Looks at her and thinks. He smiles and starts to write, holding the pencil clumsily, poking his tongue out as he concentrates.*)

Graham   Boys.

Grace   (*Smiles at* **Graham**.)

Robin   Miss?

Grace   I have a name.

Robin   Grace, you ever had a boyfriend?

Grace   Yes.

Robin   What was he like?

Grace   He bought me a box of chocolates then tried to
strangle me.

Robin   Chocolates?

Graham   That black kid?

Robin   Got a pink?

Grace   It's not about colour, colour doesn't come into it.

Robin   What was his name?

Grace   Graham.

Robin
Graham } Your boyfriend.

Grace   Paul.
Concentrate.

Robin
Graham } Do you still love him?

Grace   Please.

Robin   No but do you?

Grace   I –
No.
I never did.

Robin   Did you –

Graham   Fuck him.

Grace   Yes.
         Yes, I did do that.
         I did do that.

Robin   Oh.

Silence.
    Robin *writes.*

Robin
Graham } Gracie.

Grace   What?

Robin   If you could change one thing in your life what
         would you change?

Grace   My life.

Robin   No, one *thing* in your life.

Grace   I don't know.

Robin   No but say one thing.

Grace   Too many to choose.

Robin
Graham } But choose.

Grace   This is insane.

Robin   Wouldn't you wish your brother back?

Grace   What?

Robin   Wouldn't you wish Graham alive?

Graham
Grace } (*Laugh.*)

Grace   No. No.
         I don't think of Graham as dead.
         That's not how I think of him.

Robin   You believe in heaven?

Grace   No not at all.

Robin   Don't believe in heaven you don't believe in hell.

Grace   Can't see heaven.

Robin   I had one wish I'd wish Graham alive again.

Grace   You said change one thing in your life not have one wish.

Robin   Then I'd change Graham dead to Graham alive.

Grace   Graham's not a thing to change. And he's not in your life.

Robin   He is.

Grace   How?

Robin   They gave me his clothes.

> **Tinker** *is watching.*

Grace   It's not necessary, Robin. It's not like he's dead.

Graham }
Robin }   What would you change?

Grace   My body. So it looked like it feels.
Graham outside like Graham inside.

Robin }
Graham }   I think you've got a nice body.

Grace   I'm glad. I think you should write that word now.

Robin   My mum weren't my mum and I had to choose another, I'd choose you.

Grace   Sweet boy.

Robin   If I –
If I had to get married, I'd marry you.

Grace   No one would marry me.

Robin }
Graham }   I would.

Grace   It's not possible.

Robin   I've never kissed a girl before.

Grace   You will.

Robin   Not here I won't. Not unless it's you.

Grace   I'm not like that, a girl, no.

Robin   I don't mind.

Grace
Graham } I do.

Robin   I don't.

Grace   Listen to me. If I was going to kiss anyone here, and I'm not but if I was, it would be you.

Robin
Graham } Would it?

Grace   Definitely.
If.
But.

Robin   (*Beams and goes back to his writing.*)

A long pause.

Robin   Gracie.

Grace   Hmmn.

Robin
Graham } I love you.

Grace   I –
I love you too. But in a very particular –

Robin   Do you?

Grace   Robin, I –

Robin   Will you –

Grace
Graham } No.

Robin   Be my girlfriend?

Grace   You're a lovely boy –

Robin   I won't strangle you.

Grace   A good friend but –

Robin   I'm in love with you.

Grace   How can you be?

Robin   I just am.
I know you –

Grace   Tinker knows me.

Robin   And I love you.

Grace   Lots of people know me, they're not in love with me.

Robin }
Graham }   I am.

Grace   You're confusing me.

Robin   I only want to kiss you, won't hurt you, I swear.

Grace   When you leave –

Robin }
Graham }   Never will.

Grace   What?

Robin   Don't want to leave.

Grace   This is –

Robin   I want to be with you.

Grace   What are you saying?

Robin   I like it here.

   Tinker *enters.*
   He picks up **Robin***'s piece of paper and looks at it.*

Tinker   Fuck is that?

Robin   Flower.

Tinker   (*Sets light to the paper and burns the whole thing.*)

Robin   She smells like a flower.

Scene Eight

A patch of mud just inside the perimeter fence of the university.

It is raining.
The sound of a football match in progress on the other side of the fence.
A single rat scuttles around between **Rod** *and* **Carl**.

Rod   Baby.

Carl   (*Looks at* **Rod**. *He opens his mouth. No sound comes out.*)

Rod   You'd have watched them crucify me.

Carl   (*Tries to speak. Nothing.*
He beats the ground in frustration.)

Carl *scrabbles around in the mud and begins to write while* **Rod** *talks.*

Rod   And the rats eat my face. So what. I'd have done the same only I never said I wouldn't. You're young. I don't blame you. Don't blame yourself. No one's to blame.

Tinker *is watching.*
He lets **Carl** *finish what he is writing, then goes to him and reads it.*
He takes **Carl** *by the arms and cuts off his hands.*
Tinker *leaves.*
Carl *tries to pick up his hands – he can't, he has no hands.*
Rod *goes to* **Carl**.
He picks up the severed left hand and takes off the ring he put there.
He reads the message written in the mud.

Rod   Say you forgive me.

(*He puts on the ring.*)

I won't lie to you, Carl.

The rat begins to eat **Carl***'s right hand.*

Scene Nine

The Black Room.

Tinker *goes into his booth.*
He sits.
He puts in a token.
The flap opens.
The **Woman** *is dancing.*
Tinker *watches for a while.*

Woman   Hello, Doctor.

Tinker   Grace, I –
            Your face.

The **Woman** *sits,*
They look at each other.

Tinker   Are we friends?

Woman   Will you help me?

Tinker   I told you.

Woman   Yes.

Tinker   What should I do?

Woman   Save me.

The flap closes.
He has no more tokens.

Scene Ten

The Red Room.

Grace *is being beaten by an unseen group of men whose*
Voices *we hear.*

We hear the sound of baseball bats hitting **Grace**'s *body and she reacts as though she has received the blow.*
Graham *is watching in distress.*
Grace *is hit.*

Grace   Graham.

Voices   Dead, slag
She was having it off with her brother
Weren't he a bender?
Fucking user
All cracked up
Shit no
Shit yes
Crack crack crack

Grace *is hit once on each crack.*

Grace   Graham Jesus save me Christ

Voices   He can never (*crack*) never (*crack*) never
(*crack*) never (*crack*) never (*crack*) never
(*crack*) never (*crack*) never (*crack*) never
(*crack*) never (*crack*) never (*crack*) save
you (*crack*)

Graham   Grace.

Voices   Never (*crack*)

Stillness.
Grace *lies motionless, terrified of bringing on more blows.*

Graham   Speak to me.

Grace   (*Does not move or make a sound.*)

Graham   Can't hurt you, Grace. Can't touch you.

Grace   (*Does not move or make a sound.*)

Graham   Never.

There is a crack from nowhere, making **Grace** *scream.*

Voices   Life in the old dog yet

Graham   Switch off your head. That's what I did. Shoot
             up and switch off before the pain moves in. I
             thought of you.

There is a flurry of blows which **Grace***'s body reacts to, but she
does not make a sound.*

Graham   I used to put my spoon in my tea and heat it
             up. When you weren't looking press it on your
             skin at the top of your arm and you'd (*crack*)
             scream and I'd laugh. I'd say Do it to me.

Grace   Do it to me.

Graham   You'd press a hot spoon on me I'd not feel a
             thing.
             Knew it was coming.
             If you know it's coming you're prepared.
             If you know it's coming –

Grace   It's coming.

The blow comes.
Grace*'s body moves – not with pain, simply with the force of
the blow.*

Graham   You can surf it.

Voices   Do it to me
             Shag the slag

Grace *is raped by one of the* **Voices**.
She looks into **Graham***'s eyes throughout.*
Graham *holds her head between his hands.*

Voices   Gagging for it
             Begging for it
             Barking for it
             Arching for it
             Aching for it
             She gone?
             Not a flicker

Graham *presses his hands onto* **Grace** *and her clothes turn
red where he touches, blood seeping through.*
Simultaneously, his own body begins to bleed in the same places.

Graham   Baby baby baby.

Voices   Kill them all

A pause.
Then a long stream of automatic gunfire.
Graham *shields* **Grace***'s body with his own, and holds her*
head between his hands.
The gunfire goes on and on and on.
The wall is pitted with bullet marks, and as the gunfire continues,
huge chunks of plaster and brick are blown from the wall.
The wall is being shot to pieces and is splattered with blood.
After several minutes, the gunfire stops.
Graham *uncovers* **Grace***'s face and looks at her.*
She opens her eyes and looks at him.

Graham   No one. Nothing. Never.

Out of the ground grow daffodils.
They burst upwards, their yellow covering the entire stage.
Tinker *enters. He sees* **Grace***.*

Voices   All dead?

Tinker   Not her.

He goes to **Grace** *and kneels beside her.*
He takes her hand.

Tinker   I'm here to save you.

Graham *picks a flower and smells it.*
He smiles.

Graham   Lovely.

Scene Eleven

The Black Room.

Robin *goes into the booth that* **Tinker** *visits.*
He sits.

He puts in his one and only token.
The flap opens.
*The **Woman** is dancing.*
***Robin** watches – at first innocently eager, then bemused, then
distressed.*
She dances for sixty seconds.
The flap closes.
***Robin** sits and cries his heart out.*

Scene Twelve

The White Room.

***Grace** lies sunbathing in a tiny shaft of light coming through a
crack in the ceiling.*
***Graham** is on one side of her, **Tinker** the other.*

Tinker Whatever you want.

Grace Sun.

Graham Won't get an even tan.

Tinker Can take you there.

Grace I know.

Voices Burn you clean

Grace Hold my hand.

Graham Sunshine.

> ***Graham** takes one hand, **Tinker** the other.*

Grace My balls hurt.

Tinker You're a woman.

Voices Lunatic Grace

Grace Like to feel you here.

Graham Always be here.
And here.
And here.

Grace   (*Laughs. Then suddenly serious.*)
         They keep calling me.

Tinker   That's what I'm saying.

Graham   Love me or kill me.

Tinker   Can make you better.

Grace   Love you.

Graham   Swear.

Tinker   Yes.

Grace   On my life.

Graham   Don't cut me out.

Grace   Graham.

Voices   Frazzle it out

Tinker   Tinker.

Voices   Burn it out

Graham   Darling.

Voices   Frazzle it –

Tinker   Trust me.

Voices   Time to go

> **Tinker** *drops* **Grace**'s *hand.*
> *An electric current is switched on.*
> **Grace**'s *body is thrown into rigid shock as bits of her brain are burnt out.*
> *The shaft of light grows bigger until it engulfs them all.*
> *It becomes blinding.*

Scene Thirteen

> *The patch of mud by the perimeter fence.*
>
> *It is raining.*
> *A dozen rats share the space with* **Rod** *and* **Carl**.

Rod   If you'd said 'Me,' I wonder what would have
         happened. If he'd said 'You or Rod' and you'd said
         'Me,' I wonder if he would have killed you. He ever
         asks me I'll say 'Me. Do it to me. Not to Carl, not
         my lover, not my friend, do it to me.' I'd be gone,
         first boat out of here. Death isn't the worst thing
         they can do to you. Tinker made a man bite off
         another man's testicles. Can take away your life but
         not give you death instead.

*On the other side of the fence a child sings – Lennon and
McCartney's 'Things We Said Today.'*
Carl *and* **Rod** *listen, rapt.*
The child stops singing.
Then begins again.
Carl *stands, wobbly.*
He begins to dance – a dance of love for **Rod**.
The dance becomes frenzied, frantic, and **Carl** *makes grunting
noises, mingling with the child's singing.*
The dance loses rhythm – **Carl** *jerks and lurches out of time, his
feet sticking in the mud, a spasmodic dance of desperate regret.*
Tinker *is watching.*
He forces **Carl** *to the ground and cuts off his feet.*
He is gone.
Rod *laughs.*
The rats carry **Carl**'*s feet away.*
The child sings.

Scene Fourteen

The Black Room.

Tinker *goes to his booth.*
He tears open his trousers and sits astride the back of the chair.
He feeds a number of tokens into the slot.
The flap opens. The **Woman** *is dancing.*
Tinker *masturbates furiously until she speaks.*

Woman   Doctor.

Tinker   Don't waste my fucking time.
Sit.

Woman   (*Sits opposite* **Tinker**.)

Tinker   Open your legs.

Woman   I'm confused.

Tinker   OPEN YOUR FUCKING LEGS.

Woman   (*Does.*)

Tinker   Look.

Woman   (*Does.*)

Tinker   Touch.

Woman   (*Sobs.*)

Tinker   TOUCH FUCKING TOUCH.

Woman   Don't do this.

Tinker   YOU WANT ME TO HELP YOU?

Woman   YES

Tinker   THEN DO IT

Woman   Don't want to be this.

Tinker   You're a woman, Grace.

Woman   I want –

Tinker   Don't say that.

Woman   You said –

Tinker   I lied. You are what you are. No regrets.

Woman   Whatever I wanted.

Tinker   I'm not responsible.

Woman   Trusted you.

Tinker   Yes.

Woman   Friends.

Tinker   Don't think so.

Woman   I can change.

Tinker   You're a woman.

Woman   You're a doctor. Help me.

Tinker   No.

Woman   Is it someone else?

Tinker   No.

Woman   I love you.

Tinker   Please.

Woman   Thought you loved me.

Tinker   As you are.

Woman   Then love me, fucking love me

Tinker   Grace

Woman   Don't turn away

The flap closes.

Tinker   If I'd known –
    If I'd known.
    I've always known.

Scene Fifteen

The Round Room.

Robin *is asleep amongst a pile of books, paper and an eleven row abacus.*
He still has a pencil in his hand.
There is a box of chocolates next to his head.
Tinker *enters and stands staring at him.*
He pulls **Robin** *up by the hair.*
Robin *screams and* **Tinker** *puts a knife to his throat.*

Tinker   You fuck her?
Fuck her till her nose bleed?
I may be a cunt but I'm not a twat.

(He sees the chocolates.)

Where'd you get them?
Eh?
Eh?

Robin   They're for Grace.

Tinker   Where did you get them?

Robin   Bought them.

Tinker   What did you do, sell your arse?

Robin   *(Doesn't answer.)*

Tinker *lets go of* **Robin**.
He opens the chocolates.
He takes one out and tosses it at **Robin**.

Tinker   Eat.

Robin   *(Looks at the chocolate. He starts to cry.)*

They're for Gracie.

Tinker   Eat it.

Robin *eats the chocolate, choking on his tears.*
When he has eaten it, **Tinker** *tosses him another.*
Robin *eats it, sobbing.*
Tinker *throws him another.*
Robin *eats it.*
Tinker *throws him another.*
Robin *eats it.*
Tinker *throws him another.*
Robin *eats it.*
Tinker *throws him another.*
Robin *eats it.*
Tinker *throws him another.*
Robin *eats it.*
Tinker *throws him another.*

Robin *eats it.*
Tinker *throws him another.*
Robin *eats it.*
Tinker *throws him another.*
Robin *eats it.*
Tinker *throws him another.*
Robin *eats it.*
Tinker *tosses him the last chocolate.*
Robin *retches. Then eats the chocolate.*
Tinker *takes the empty tray out of the box – there is another layer of chocolates underneath.*
Tinker *throws* **Robin** *a chocolate.*
Robin *eats it.*
Tinker *throws him another.*
Robin *eats it.*
Tinker *throws him another.*
Robin *eats it.*
Tinker *throws him another.*
Robin *eats it.*
Tinker *throws him another.*
Robin *eats it.*
Tinker *throws him another.*
Robin *eats it.*
Tinker *throws him another.*
Robin *eats it.*
Tinker *throws him another.*
Robin *eats it.*
Tinker *throws him another.*
Robin *eats it.*
Tinker *throws him another.*
Robin *eats it.*
Tinker *throws him another.*
Robin *eats it.*
Tinker *tosses him the last chocolate.*
Robin *eats it.*
Tinker *throws the empty box at him, then notices that* **Robin** *has wet himself.*

Tinker   Filthy little perv, clean it up.

Robin *stands in the puddle, distressed.*
Tinker *grabs* **Robin***'s head and forces it down, rubbing his face in his own urine.*

Tinker   Clean it up, woman.

Robin *looks around in a panic.*
He tries to use the empty chocolate box to clean up the urine, but it spreads it around.
He tears up some nearby books and soaks up the mess.
He looks at the books, distraught.

Robin   Gracie.

Tinker   (*Tosses* **Robin** *a box of matches.*)

Robin   (*Looks at* **Tinker**.)

Tinker   (*Looks back at* **Robin**.)

Robin   (*Piles up the spoiled books and burns them.*)

Tinker   All of them.

Robin *burns as many books as he can and watches them go up in flames.*
Grace *enters, vacant and tranquillized, with* **Graham**.
She watches.
Robin *smiles nervously.*

Robin   Sorry. I was cold.

Graham *leads* **Grace** *towards the fire.*
She warms her hands from the heat of the flames.

Grace   Lovely.

Scene Sixteen

The patch of mud by the perimeter fence.

Scorching heat.
The sound of fire.
Most of the rats are dead.
The few that remain are running around frantically.

Rod   There's only now.

   (*He cries.*)

Carl   (*Hugs him.*)

Rod   That's all there's ever been.

   Carl *kisses him.*
   He makes love to **Rod**.

Rod   I will always love you.
   I will never lie to you.
   I will never betray you.
   On my life.

   They both come.
   Rod *takes off the ring and puts it in* **Carl**'s *mouth.*
   Carl *swallows it. He cries.*
   They hug tightly, then go to sleep wrapped around each other.
   Tinker *is watching.*
   He pulls **Rod** *away from* **Carl**.

Tinker   You or him, Rod, what's it to be?

Rod   Me. Not Carl. Me.

Tinker   (*Cuts* **Rod**'s *throat.*)

Carl   (*Struggles to get to* **Rod**. *He is held.*)

Rod   It can't be this.

   (*He dies.*)

Tinker   Burn him.

Scene Seventeen

   The Round Room.

   Robin, **Grace** *and* **Graham** *are by the ashes of the fire.*
   Grace *is still rubbing her hands slowly and holding them up as
   if it were ablaze.*
   Robin *retrieves his abacus from the ashes.*

He holds it up to **Grace**.
She doesn't respond.

Robin   Been working on the numbers. Think I've cracked
             it.

Grace   (*Doesn't respond.*)

Robin   Shall I show you?

Grace   (*Doesn't respond.*)

Robin   Right, I'll –
             Days left. Try that.

             (*He counts off the beads on a single row.*)

             One. Two. Three. Four. Five. Six. Seven.

             (*He stares at the seven beads, then slowly moves one bead
             on the next row along.*)

             One.

             (*He counts off the beads on rows three to eight.*)

             One. Two. Three. Four. Five. Six. Seven. Eight.
             Nine. Ten. Eleven. Twelve. Thirteen. Fourteen.
             Fifteen. Sixteen. Seventeen. Eighteen. Nineteen.
             Twenty. Twenty-one. Twenty-two. Twenty-three.
             Twenty-four. Twenty-five. Twenty-six. Twenty-
             seven. Twenty-eight. Twenty-nine. Thirty. Thirty-
             one. Thirty-two. Thirty-three. Thirty-four. Thirty-
             five. Thirty-six. Thirty-seven. Thirty-eight. Thirty-
             nine. Forty. Forty-one. Forty-two. Forty-three.
             Forty-four. Forty-five. Forty-six. Forty-seven. Forty-
             eight. Forty-nine. Fifty. Fifty-one. Fifty-two.

             (*He stares at the beads.*)

             Fifty-two sevens.

             (*He slowly moves one bead on the next row along.*)

             One.

             (*He counts off the beads on the last three rows.*)

One. Two. Three. Four. Five. Six. Seven. Eight.
Nine. Ten. Eleven. Twelve. Thirteen. Fourteen.
Fifteen. Sixteen. Seventeen. Eighteen. Nineteen.
Twenty. Twenty-one. Twenty-two. Twenty-three.
Twenty-four. Twenty-five. Twenty-six. Twenty-seven. Twenty-eight. Twenty-nine. Thirty.

Thirty fifty-two sevens.

(*He looks at* **Grace**.)

Thirty fifty-two sevens.

Gracie?

Grace   (*Doesn't respond.*)

Robin *takes off his tights (**Grace**'s) and makes a noose.*
He gets a chair and stands on it.
He attaches the noose to the ceiling and puts his head through.
He stands in silence for a few moments.

Robin   Grace.
Grace.
Grace.
Grace.
Grace.
Grace.
Please, Miss.

The chair is pulled from under **Robin**.
He struggles.
Tinker *is watching.*

Graham   He's dying, Grace.

Grace   (*Doesn't respond.*)

Graham *looks at* **Robin**.
Robin *looks at* **Graham** – *he sees him.*
Still choking, **Robin** *holds out a hand to* **Graham**.
Graham *takes it.*
Then wraps his arms around **Robin**'s *legs and pulls.*
Robin *dies.*
Graham *sits under* **Robin**'s *swinging feet.*
Tinker *goes to* **Grace** *and takes her hand.*

Tinker   Say good night to the folks, Gracie.

He leads her off.
Graham *sits motionless under* **Robin**'s *swinging body.*

Scene Eighteen

The White Room.

Grace *lies unconscious on a bed.*
She is naked apart from a tight strapping around her groin and chest, and blood where her breasts should be.
Carl *lies unconscious next to her. He is naked apart from a bloodied bandage strapped around his groin.*
Tinker *stands between them.*
Tinker *undoes* **Grace**'s *bandage and looks at her groin.*
Grace *stirs.*

Grace   F– F–

Tinker   What you wanted, I hope you –

Grace   F– F– F–

Tinker *helps* **Grace** *up and leads her to the mirror.*
Graham *enters.*
Grace *focuses on the mirror.*
She opens her mouth.

Graham   It's over.

Tinker   Nice-looking lad.
Like your brother.
I hope you –
What you wanted.

Grace   (*Touches her stitched-on genitals.*)

F– F–

Tinker   Do you like it?

Grace   F–

Tinker   You'll get used to him.
Can't call you Grace any more.
Call you . . . Graham. I'll call you Graham.

(*He begins to leave.*)

Graham   Tinker.

Tinker   (*Turns and looks at* **Grace**.)

Grace
Graham } Felt it.

Tinker   I'm sorry. I'm not really a doctor.

(*He kisses* **Grace** *very gently.*)

Tinker
Graham } Goodbye, Grace.

> **Tinker** and **Graham** *both turn away.*
> *They leave.*
> **Grace** *stares at the mirror.*
> **Carl** *sits up in bed and opens his mouth.*
> *He looks at* **Grace**. *She looks at him.*
> **Carl** *lets out a silent scream.*

Scene Nineteen

The Black Room.

> **Tinker** *enters and sits.*
> *He feeds the viewing mechanism.*
> *The flap opens.*
> *The* **Woman** *is dancing.*
> *She stops and sits.*

Woman   Hello, Tinker.

Tinker   Hello, my love.

Woman   How are you?

Tinker   She's gone.

Woman   Who?

A long silence.

Woman   Can I kiss you?

Tinker   (*Smiles.*)

> *The **Woman** opens the partition and comes through to
> **Tinker**'s side.*
> *She kisses him.*
> *He hesitates.*
> *She kisses him again.*
> *He kisses her.*
> *He looks down at the floor.*

Tinker   I'm confused.

Woman   I know.

Tinker   I think I –
Misunderstood.

Woman   I know. You're beautiful.

Tinker   Grace, she –

Woman   I know. I love you.

> *They look at each other.*
> *She kisses him.*
> *He responds.*
> *She takes off her top.*
> *He looks at her breasts.*
> *He takes her right breast into his mouth.*

Woman   I think about you when I . . .
And wish it was you when I . . . .

Tinker   (*Withdraws and looks at her.*)

Most glorious fucking breasts I ever met.

Woman   Make love to me, Tinker.

Tinker   Are you sure?

Woman   Make love to me.

They both undress, watching each other.
They stand naked and look at each other's bodies.
They slowly embrace.
They begin to make love very slowly.

Woman   (*Cries.*)

Tinker   (*Stops.*) You all right? We can –

Woman   No, no I –

Tinker   Does it hurt do you want me to stop?

He begins to withdraw – she holds on to him.

Woman   Stay there. Stay there.
I love you.

They begin to make love again, very gently.
Tinker *begins to cry.*
The **Woman** *licks away his tears.*

Woman   I love your cock, Tinker
I love your cock inside me, Tinker
Fuck me, Tinker
Harder, harder, harder
Come inside me
I love you, Tinker

Tinker   (*Comes.*)

Sorry.

Woman   No.

Tinker   I couldn't –

Woman   I know.

Tinker   Fuck me fuck me fuck me I love you I love you
I love you why have you come?

Woman   (*Laughs.*) I know. My fault.

Tinker   No, I –

Woman   It's all right.
I love you.
Plenty of time.

They hold each other, him inside her, not moving.

Woman Are you here?

Tinker Yes.

Woman Now.

Tinker Yes.

Woman With me.

Tinker Yes.

Pause.

Tinker What's your name?

Woman Grace.

Tinker No, I meant –

Woman I know. It's Grace.

Tinker (*Smiles.*) I love you, Grace.

Scene Twenty

The patch of mud by the perimeter fence.

It is raining.
Carl and **Grace** *sit next to each other.*
Grace *now looks and sounds exactly like* **Graham**. *She is wearing his clothes.*
Carl *wears* **Robin**'s *clothes, that is,* **Grace**'s *(women's) clothes.*
There are two rats, one chewing at **Grace/Graham**'s *wounds, the other at* **Carl**'s.

Grace/Graham Body perfect.

Chain-smoked all day but danced like a dream you'd never know.

Have they done it yet?

Died.

Burnt.

Lump of charred meat stripped of its clothes.

Back to life.

Why don't you ever say anything?

Loved

Me

Hear a voice or catch a smile turning from the mirror You bastard how dare you leave me like this.

Felt it.
Here. Inside. Here.

And when I don't feel it, it's pointless.
Think about getting up it's pointless.
Think about eating it's pointless.
Think about dressing it's pointless.
Think about speaking it's pointless.
Think about dying only it's totally fucking pointless.

Here now.
Safe on the other side and here.

Graham.

(*A long silence.*)

Always be here.
Thank you, Doctor.

Grace/Graham *looks at* **Carl**.
Carl *is crying.*

Grace/Graham   Help me.

Carl *reaches out his arm.*
Grace/Graham *holds his stump.*

They stare at the sky, **Carl** *crying.*
It stops raining.
The sun comes out.
Grace/Graham *smiles.*
The sun gets brighter and brighter, the squeaking of the rats louder
and louder, until the light is blinding and the sound deafening.

Blackout.

Crave

My thanks to Vicky Featherstone, Alan Westaway, Catherine Cusack, Andrew Maud, Kathryn Howdon, Mel Kenyon, Nils Tabert, Domingo Ledezma, Jelena Pejíc, Elana Greenfield and New Dramatists.

For Mark.

Crave was premiered by Paines Plough at the Traverse Theatre, Edinburgh on 13 August 1998. The cast was as follows:

C Sharon Duncan-Brewster
M Ingrid Craigie
B Paul Thomas Hickey
A Alan Williams

Director   Vicky Featherstone
Designer   Georgia Sion
Lighting by   Nigel J. Edwards

Characters

C
M
B
A

Author's note

Punctuation is used to indicate delivery, not to conform to the rules of grammar.

A stroke (/) indicates the point of interruption in overlapping dialogue.

Editor's note

This edition of *Crave*, first reprinted in 2000, incorporates minor revisions made to the original text by Sarah Kane shortly before her death. It should therefore be regarded as the definitive version in all respects.

C You're dead to me.

B My will reads, Fuck this up and I'll haunt you for the rest of your fucking life.

C He's following me.

A What do you want?

B To die.

C Somewhere outside the city, I told my mother, You're dead to me.

B No that's not it.

C If I could be free of you without having to lose you.

A Sometimes that's not possible.

M I keep telling people I'm pregnant. They say How did you do it, what are you taking? I say I drank a bottle of port, smoked some fags and fucked a stranger.

B All lies.

C He needs to have a secret but he can't help telling. He thinks we don't know. Believe me, we know.

M A voice in the desert.

C He who comes after.

M There is something in the way.

A Still here.

C Three summers ago I was bereaved. No one died but I lost my mother.

A She had him back.

C I believe in anniversaries. That a mood can be repeated even if the event that caused it is trivial or forgotten. In this case it's neither.

M I will grow older and I will, it will, something

B I smoke till I'm sick.

A   Black on white and blue.

C   When I wake I think my period must have started or rather never stopped because it only finished three days ago.

M   The heat is going out of me.

C   The heart is going out of me.

B   I feel nothing, nothing.
I feel nothing.

M   Is it possible?

B   Sorry?

A   I'm not a rapist.

M   David?

   A beat.

B   Yeah.

A   I'm a paedophile.

M   Do you remember me?

   A beat.

B   Yeah.

C   Looks like a German,

A   Talks like a Spaniard,

C   Smokes like a Serb.

M   You've forgotten.

C   All things to all men.

B   I don't think

M   Yes.

C   I couldn't forget.

M   I looked for you. All over the city.

B   I really don't

M Yes. Yes.

A You do.

M Yes.

C Please stop this.

M And now I have found you.

C Someone has died who is not dead.

A And now we are friends.

C It's not my fault, it was never my fault.

M Everything that happens is supposed to happen.

B Where you been?

M Here and there.

C Leave.

B Where?

C Now.

M There.

A Because love by its nature desires a future.

C If she'd left –

M I want a child.

B I can't help you.

C None of this would have happened.

M Time is passing and I don't have time.

C None of it.

B No.

C None.

A In a lay-by on the motorway going out of the city, or maybe in, depending on which way you look, a small dark girl sits in the passenger seat of a parked car. Her elderly grandfather undoes his trousers and it pops out of his pants, big and purple.

C I feel nothing, nothing.
I feel nothing.

A And when she cries, her father in the back seat says I'm sorry, she's not normally like this.

M Haven't we been here before?

A And though she cannot remember she cannot forget.

C And has been hurtling away from that moment ever since.

B Will you come round and seduce me? I need to be seduced by an older woman.

M I'm not an older woman.

B Older than me, not older *per se.*

C You've fallen in love with someone that doesn't exist.

A Tragedy.

B Really.

M Oh yes.

A What do you want?

C To die.

B To sleep.

M No more.

A And the bus driver loses it, stops the bus in the middle of the road, climbs out of his cab, strips off his clothes and walks down the street, his cute little arse shining in the sun.

B I drink till I'm sick.

C Everywhere I go, I see him. I know the plates, I know the car, does he think I don't know?

A   You're never as powerful as when you know you're powerless.

B   I shake when I don't have it.

M   Bleeding.

B   Brain melts when I do.

M   I ran through the poppy field at the back of my grandfather's farm. When I burst in through the kitchen door I saw him sitting with my grandmother on his lap. He kissed her on the lips and caressed her breast. They looked around and saw me, smiling at my confusion. When I related this to my mother more than ten years later she stared at me oddly and said 'That didn't happen to you. It happened to me. My father died before you were born. When that happened I was pregnant with you, but I didn't know it until the day of his funeral.'

C   We pass these messages.

M   Someone somewhere is crying for me, crying for my death.

B   My fingers inside her, my tongue in her mouth.

C   I wish to live with myself.

A   No witnesses.

M   And if this makes no sense then you understand perfectly.

A   It's not what you think.

C   No that's not it.

M   Time after time, same fucking excuse.

C   LEAVE.

A   COME BACK.

All   STAY.

C   Can't have this again.

A   Stunned.

B Stoned.

M I have a black black side I know. I have a side so green you will never know.

B Have another drink, another cigarette.

M Sometimes the shape of my head alarms me. When I catch sight of it reflected in a darkened train window, the landscape passing through the image of my head. Not that there is anything unusual or . . . alarming . . . about the shape of my head, but it does . . . alarm me.

A Why do you do this?

C I find it alarming.

M There's so little time.

C I hate the smell of my own family.

B Base 1.
Base 2.
Base 3.
Bingo.

C You'll smell better when you're dead than you do now.

A An American woman translated a novel from Spanish into English. She asked her Spanish classmate his opinion of her work. The translation was very bad. He said he would help her and she offered to pay him for his time. He refused. She offered to take him out to dinner. This was acceptable to him so he agreed. But she forgot. The Spaniard is still waiting for his dinner.

B El dinero viene solo.

C Alone.

M If love would come.

B It's just not me.

A Has it ever occurred to you you're looking in the wrong place?

M Now.

B Never.

C No.

B It's very nice. Will you make me one?

M It's made of egg shells and concrete.

B Will you make me one?

M Concrete, paint and egg shells.

B I didn't ask what it was made of, I asked if you'd make me one.

M Every time I have an egg I stick the shell on there and spray it.

C She sees through walls.

B Will. You. Make. Me. One.

C Other lives.

A A mother beats her child savagely because it runs out in front of a car.

M You stop thinking of yourself as I, you think of we.

B Let's just go to/bed.

C no no no no no no no no no

A A wish under pressure.

C Cry blue murder.

M Do not remove your gloves until you leave the last town.

B Are you a lesbian?

M Oh please.

B I thought that might be why you don't have children.

A Why?

M I never met a man I trusted.

C Why what?

B You trust me?

M This has nothing to do with you.

C Why what?

M I'm not interested in you.

C Why what, why what?

M I'm not interested in the first fucking thing about you.

A I don't drink. I hate smoking. I'm vegetarian. I don't fuck around. I've never visited a prostitute and I've never had a sexually transmitted disease other than thrush. This does, I'm afraid, make me a rarity, if not unique.

B Look.

C Listen.

B Look. My nose.

M What about it.

B What do you think?

C Broken.

B I've never broken a bone in my body.

A Like Christ.

B But my Dad has. Smashed his nose in a car crash when he was eighteen. And I've got this. Genetically impossible, but there it is. We pass these messages faster than we think and in ways we don't think possible.

C If I was
     If I
     If I was

M HURRY UP PLEASE IT'S TIME

B And don't you think that a child conceived by rape would suffer?

C   But as it is.

M   You think I'm going to rape you?

C   Yes.

A   No.

B   Yes.

M   No.

A   No.

B   Yes.

C   Yes.

M   Is that possible?

C   I see no good in anyone any more.

B   Okay, I was, okay, I was, okay okay. I was, okay, two people, right?

A   Okay.

B   One of these days,

C   Soon very soon,

M   Now.

A   But looks aren't everything.

B   It's just not me.

A   A small boy had an imaginary friend. He took her to the beach and they played in the sea. A man came from the water and took her away. The following morning the body of a girl was found washed up on the beach.

M   What's that got to do with anything?

A   Clutching a fistful of sand.

B   Everything.

C   What's anything got to do with anything?

M   Nothing.

A   Exactly.

B   That's the worst of it.

M   Nothing.

C   Is this what it is?
Is this it?

M   How much longer

B   How many more times

A   How much more

C   Corrupt or inept.

B   I am nobody's windfall.

A   I'm sorry.

C   Go away.

M   Now.

C   Go away.

B   I'm sorry.

C   Go away.

A   I'm sorry, I'm sorry, I'm sorry, I'm sorry, I'm sorry, I'm sorry, I'm sorry.

C   What for?

M   Have you ever raped anyone?

A   I'm sorry I'm following you.

B   No.

M   Why not?

A   There're worse things than being fat and fifty.

M   Why not?

A   Being dead and thirty.

M I'm the kind of woman about whom people say Who *was* that woman?

A The question is Where do you live and where do you want to live?

M Absence sleeps between the buildings at night.

C Don't die.

B This city, fucking love it, wouldn't live nowhere else, couldn't.

M Where do you find it?

C Where do I start?

A A Japanese man in love with his virtual reality girlfriend.

B You look reasonably happy for someone who's not.

M Where do I stop?

A Swords in turmoil.

B Here.

C I'm looking for a time and place free of things that crawl, fly or sting.

M Inside.

A Here.

M Be the one.

C If she'd left –

M I don't want to grow old and cold and be too poor to dye my hair.

C You get mixed messages because I have mixed feelings.

M I don't want to be living in a bedsit at sixty, too scared to turn the heater on because I can't pay the bill.

C What ties me to you is guilt.

M I don't want to die alone and not be found till my bones are clean and the rent overdue.

C I don't want to stay.

B I don't want to stay.

C I want you to leave.

M If love would come.

A Let it happen.

C No.

M It's leaving me behind.

B No.

C No.

M Yes.

B No.

A Yes.

C No.

M Yes.

B Let me go.

C I don't want to have to buy you Christmas presents any more.

B Just a name would be nice.

M You're very naïve if you think you still have those kind of choices.

B My back aches.

C My head aches.

A My heart aches.

M You shouldn't sleep next to the radiator.

B Where should I sleep?

M Do you want a massage?

C Don't touch me.

M   I shouldn't be doing this.

A   One touch.

B   Will you get into trouble?

A   An isolated act.

M   No, I . . . mustn't get attached.

A   It's only natural.

B   Seeing another human being in distress.

C   I feel
I just feel

M   You asked me to seduce you.

B   Not tie me up.

A   Be grateful.

C   As a child I liked to piss on the carpet.
The carpet rotted and I blamed it on the dog.

M   I'm unable to know you.

C   Don't want to know me.

M   Utterly unknowable.

A   Still here.

M   I need a child.

B   That's all?

C   It's everything.

M   That's all.

B   Meni ni iz džepa, ni u džep.

C   Mother.

A   The king is dead, long live the king.

B   If it could be an act of love.

C   I can't remember

B   Whose

C   Any more

A   Why do you think that is?

C   My mind's a blank.

M   Why are you laughing?

C   Someone has died.

B   You think I'm laughing?

M   Why are you crying?

C   You're dead to me.

B   You think I'm crying?

C   I'll cry if you laugh.

B   You could be my mother.

M   I'm not your mother.

A   Baby.

M   now now now now now now now

C   Am I an unnecessary complication?

B   A sporadic addict.

A   No one but you.

B   Addicted to sickness.

A   It's not you, it's me.

C   It's always me.

A   I want to sleep next to you and do your shopping and carry your bags and tell you how much I love being with you but they keep making me do stupid things.

M   It's not me, it's you.

B   Pointless fucking

M   Time sheet.

C   Six month plan.

A   And I want to play hide-and-seek and give you my
clothes and tell you I like your shoes and sit on the steps
while you take a bath and massage your neck and kiss
your feet and hold your hand and go for a meal and not
mind when you eat my food and meet you at Rudy's and
talk about the day and type up your letters and carry your
boxes and laugh at your paranoia and give you tapes you
don't listen to and watch great films and watch terrible
films and complain about the radio and take pictures of
you when you're sleeping and get up to fetch you coffee
and bagels and Danish and go to Florent and drink coffee
at midnight and have you steal my cigarettes and never
be able to find a match and tell you about the tv
programme I saw the night before and take you to the
eye hospital and not laugh at your jokes and want you in
the morning but let you sleep for a while and kiss your
back and stroke your skin and tell you how much I love
your hair your eyes your lips your neck your breasts your
arse your

and sit on the steps smoking till your neighbour comes
home and sit on the steps smoking till *you* come home
and worry when you're late and be amazed when you're
early and give you sunflowers and go to your party and
dance till I'm black and be sorry when I'm wrong and
happy when you forgive me and look at your photos and
wish I'd known you forever and hear your voice in my
ear and feel your skin on my skin and get scared when
you're angry and your eye has gone red and the other
eye blue and your hair to the left and your face oriental
and tell you you're gorgeous and hug you when you're
anxious and hold you when you hurt and want you when
I smell you and offend you when I touch you and
whimper when I'm next to you and whimper when I'm
not and dribble on your breast and smother you in the
night and get cold when you take the blanket and hot
when you don't and melt when you smile and dissolve
when you laugh and not understand why you think I'm

rejecting you when I'm not rejecting you and wonder
how you could think I'd ever reject you and wonder who
you are but accept you anyway and tell you about the
tree angel enchanted forest boy who flew across the
ocean because he loved you and write poems for you and
wonder why you don't believe me and have a feeling so
deep I can't find words for it and want to buy you a
kitten I'd get jealous of because it would get more
attention than me and keep you in bed when you have to
go and cry like a baby when you finally do and get rid of
the roaches and buy you presents you don't want and
take them away again and ask you to marry me and you
say no *again* but keep on asking because though you think
I don't mean it I do always have from the first time I
asked you and wander the city thinking it's empty
without you and want what you want and think I'm
losing myself but know I'm safe with you and tell you the
worst of me and try to give you the best of me because
you don't deserve any less and answer your questions
when I'd rather not and tell you the truth when I really
don't want to and try to be honest because I know you
prefer it and think it's all over but hang on in for just ten
more minutes before you throw me out of your life and
forget who I am and try to get closer to you because it's
beautiful learning to know you and well worth the effort
and speak German to you badly and Hebrew to you
worse and make love with you at three in the morning
and somehow somehow somehow communicate
some of the/overwhelming undying overpowering
unconditional all-encompassing heart-enriching
mind-expanding on-going never-ending love I have
for you.

C   (*Under her breath until* **A** *stops speaking.*) this has to stop this
has to stop this has to stop this has to stop this has to stop
this has to stop this has to stop this has to stop (*Then at
normal volume.*) this has to stop this has to stop this has
to stop

A   Don't they *understand?* I've got *important* things to do.

C   It's getting worse.

A   I am lost, so fucking lost in this mess of a woman.

B   She wants a kid yesterday.

A   What will I do when you throw me away?

C   Listen.

B   Look.

C   Listen. I am here to remember. I need to . . . remember.
I have this grief and I don't know why.

A   You're always gorgeous, but you're particularly gorgeous
when you come.

C   That violent terrified paralysed child.

A   As she gets more and more angry off come more and more
clothes as it gets less and less likely she'll let me
anywhere near her.

B   I have a bad bad feeling about this bad bad feeling.

A   I am so lonely, so fucking lonely.

C   I didn't

A   I don't

C   Understand

M   Control, control, relax and control.

A   It is this woman with the desolate eyes for whom I would
die.

C   Her hair is white, but for some reason – perhaps because
her hair is white – I have no idea how old she is.

M   Sunny landscapes. Pastel walls. Gentle air conditioning.

A   I keep trying to understand but I don't.

C   I look at the large beige hessian cushion, try to connect, try
to decipher myself woven into the clean blank fabric.

A   When does it stop?

C   And then at the paisley green cushion, a thoroughly inappropriate cushion to represent any part of me, especially the parts I am showing to her.

M   Do you have difficulty in relationships with men?

A   busy happy busy happy busy happy

M   Do you *have* relationships with men?

B   The only thing I want to say I've said already, and it's a bit fucking tedious to say it again, no matter how true it is, no matter that it's the one unifying thought humanity has.

A   HOW CAN YOU LEAVE ME LIKE THIS?

C   My grief has nothing to do with men. I'm having a breakdown because I'm going to die.

A   Long before I had the chance to adore all of you, I adored the bits of you I could see.

B   The woman with dragon eyes.

A   Blue into green.

C   All blue.

A   I don't have music, Christ I wish I had music but all I have is words.

B   Du bist die Liebe meines Lebens.

A   Don't cut me out.

B   Something inside me that kicks like a bastard.

C   A dull ache in my solar plexus.

B   Gag for a fag.

M   Have you ever been hospitalised?

A   Pain by association.

C   I need a miracle to save me.

M What for?

A Insanity.

C Anorexia. Bulimia.

B Whatever.

C No.

M Never.

C Sorry.

A The truth is simple.

C I'm evil, I'm damaged, and no one can save me.

A Death is an option.

B I disgust myself.

C Depression's inadequate. A full scale emotional collapse is the minimum required to justify letting everyone down.

A The coward's way out,

C I don't have the courage.

B I think about you

A Dream about you

B Talk about you

A Can't get you out of my system.

M It's okay.

B I like you in my system.

M No performance needed.

C One fine morning in the month of May.

B No that's not it.

C You could be my mother.

M I'm not your mother.

C   I have this guilt and I don't know why.

A   Only love can save me and love has destroyed me.

C   A field. A basement. A bed. A car.

B   In a day or two I'll go back for another affair, although the affair is now so on-going it almost constitutes a relationship.

M   Go on.

B   If you don't want me to come I won't come. You can say, it doesn't matter. I mean it matters but it's better to say. Then I'll know. So.

M   Beyond the pale.

A   Beyond the pain.

M   Choose, focus, apply.

B   I fancy my chances.

C   I buy a new tape recorder and blank tapes.

B   I always do.

C   I have old ones that will do just as well in actuality, but the truth has little to do with actuality, and the point (if there is one) is to record the truth.

A   I am so tired.

C   I crave white on white and black, but my thoughts race in glorious technicolour, prodding me awake, whipping away the warm blanket of invisibility every time it swears to smother my mind in nothing.

A   Most people,

B   They get on,

A   They get up,

B   They get on.

A   My hollow heart is full of darkness.

C   One touch record.

M   Filled with emptiness.

B   Satisfied with nothing.

A   One touch.

M   Record.

C   My bowel curls at his touch.

A   Poor, poor love.

C   I feel nothing, nothing.
I feel nothing.

B   I came back.

C   If she'd left –

A   I'm going to die.

M   This abuse has gone on long enough.

C   Maggots everywhere.

B   There's no one like you.

C   Whenever I look really close at something, it swarms with white larvae.

A   Black folding in.

C   I open my mouth and I too am full of them, crawling down my throat.

B   Something happened.

A   So aghast.

C   I try to pull it out but it gets longer and longer, there's no end to it. I swallow it and pretend it isn't there.

B   Imperceptibly slowly and in an instant.

A   Nothing spectacular.

B   I keep coming back.

A A horror so deep only ritual can contain it,

M Express it,

B Explain it,

A Maintain it.

B Besos brujos que me matan.

C The navy denim dress I wore at six, the elastic red and blue belt tight round my waist, nylon socks, the hard crust of scabs on my knees, the metal barred climbing frame between my legs, David –

A NO.

M I cannot love you because I cannot respect you.

C Clean slate, long love.

M I was catching a plane. A psychic predicted that I would not get on this flight but that my lover would. The plane would crash and he would be killed. I didn't know what to do. If I missed the flight I would be fulfilling the prophecy so risking my lover's death. But in order to break the prophecy I would have to get on a plane which seemed destined to crash.

A What did you do?

M Begin again.

A Begin again.

C Purple heather scratching my legs.

A Anything but this.

C A handsome blond fourteen year old, his thumbs hooked over his jeans half exposing his buttocks, his blue blue eyes full of the sun.

B Sick of it, man, I'm totally fucking sick of it.

A What did you do?

B Nothing, nothing, I did nothing.

M None of this matters because I'm simply not in love
with you.

A And I am shaking, sobbing with the memory of her, when
she loved me, before I was her torturer, before there was
no room in me for her, before we misunderstood, in fact
the very first moment I saw her, her eyes smiling and full
of the sun, and I shudder with grief for that moment which
I've been hurtling away from ever since.

B Begin again, begin again.

M Move on.

A I look at her breast,

C A balloon of milk,

M Sooner or later,

C A bubble of blood,

B One way or another,

C Gurgling blood,

B That is going into my mouth,

C Thick yellow blood,

A My pain is nothing compared to hers.

C but but but

A (and this is crucial)

B Don't say no to me.

C I keep coming back.

B You have this effect.

M You can't say no.

A Dark angel divine.

C It's not him I want.

A I fucking miss you.

C   It's my virginity.

B   I miss fucking you.

C   A fourteen year old to steal my virginity on the moor and rape me till I come.

M   One of these days

B   Soon very soon

A   Love you till then

M   (and after?)

C   I have children, the men come, I am fighting but they take them, I realise, the men, they came, they said, in the night, they said

A   don't say no to me you can't say no to me because it's such a relief to have love again and to lie in bed and be held and touched and kissed and adored and your heart will leap when you hear my voice and see my smile and feel my breath on your neck and your heart will race when I want to see you and I will lie to you from day one and use you and screw you and break your heart because you broke mine first and you will love me more each day until the weight is unbearable and your life is mine and you'll die alone because I will take what I want then walk away and owe you nothing it's always there it's always been there and you cannot deny the life you feel fuck that life fuck that life fuck that life I have lost you now

C   GOT ME

B   Now I have found you I can stop looking for myself.

C   She touched my arm and smiled.

B   One of those faces I could never have imagined.

A   We checked into a hotel pretending we weren't going to have sex.

C   Eyes, whispers, shades and shadows.

M Where you going who you seeing what you doing?

B Jebem radoznale.

A I have to be where I want to be.

M Can't have this again.

A We made love, then she threw up.

C No one to help me not my fucking mother neither.

A I crossed two rivers and wept by one.

M I close my eyes and I see her close her eyes and she sees you.

A The scream of a daffodil,

M The stain of a scream.

C I watched my father beat my mother with a walking stick.

A A stain,

C An echo,

A A stain.

B I'm sorry you saw that.

C I'm sorry he did it.

A I despair of despair.

M No regrets.

A I swear I can't bear to look at you.

C I did nothing, nothing.

B I did nothing.

C I want to feel physically like I feel emotionally.
Starved.

M Beaten.

A Broken.

C He buys me a make-up kit, blushers and lipstick and eyeshadow. And I paint my face in bruises and blood and cuts and swelling, and on the mirror in deep red, UGLY.

A Death is my lover and he wants to move in.

B What does that mean, what does that mean, what does that mean what you're saying?

C Be a woman, be a woman, FUCK YOU.

M There's something very unflattering about being desired when the other person is so drunk they can't see.

B Fuck you.

C I tried to explain that I don't want to sleep with someone who won't appreciate how hard it was for me the following morning, but he'd passed out by the time I finished my sentence.

M QED.

C Still sleeping with Daddy.

A The games we play,

M The lies we tell.

B Your hair is an act of God.

A A Vietnamese girl, her entire existence given meaning and permanence in the thirty seconds she fled from her village, skin melting, mouth open.

C No one can hate me more than I hate myself.

A I am not what I am, I am what I do.

M This is terrible.

C This is true.

A The thing I swore I'd never do, the thing I swore I'd –

M All that pain

C Forever

B Till now.

A   On my children's lives, my children's love.

M   Why do you drink so much?

B   The fags aren't killing me fast enough.

C   My laughter is a bubble of despair.

M   Rule one.

C   No records.

M   No letters.

A   No credit card bills for afternoons in hotel rooms, no receipts for expensive jewellery, no calling at home then hanging up in silence.

C   No feeling,

B   No emotion,

M   A cold fuck and a goldfish memory.

C   My bowels gave way.

A   Throbbing between shame and guilt.

C   Mess. Mess.

A   She knows.

B   It's just not me.

A   Never keep souvenirs of a murder.

M   Everything's clear.

C   Another girl,

B   Another life.

C   I did nothing, nothing.

B   I did nothing.

M   Beyond the pale.

A   God forgive me I want to be clean.

C   He screams at me to see what I have become.

M　Go on.

C　Why can no one make love to me the way I want to be loved?

M　I could be your mother.

B　You're not my mother.

M　Soon very soon.

B　Now.

C　I've faked orgasms before, but this is the first time I've faked *not* having an orgasm.

A　From under the door seeps a black pool of blood.

M　Why?

C　What?

B　Why what?

A　What?

M　When he's generous, kind, thoughtful and happy, I know he's having an affair.

C　He thinks we're stupid, he thinks we don't know.

M　A third person in my bed whose face eludes me.

B　Just me,

A　Just the way I am,

C　Nothing to be done.

M　Give, sympathise, control.

B　Now.

C　So tired of secrets.

M　It's just not me.

C　She is currently having some kind of nervous breakdown and wishes she'd been born black, male and more attractive.

B I give myself.

C Or just more attractive.

B I give my heart.

C Or just different.

M But that's not really giving.

C Just someone fucking else.

A Fragile and choking.

C She ceases to continue with the day to day farce of getting through the next few hours in an attempt to ward off the fact that she doesn't know how to get through the next forty years.

A I love you still,

B Against my will.

C She's talking about herself in the third person because the idea of being who she is, of acknowledging that she is herself, is more than her pride can take.

B With a fucking vengeance.

C She's sick to the fucking gills of herself and wishes wishes wishes that something would happen to make life begin.

A I'm a much nicer person since I had an affair.

C You can only kill yourself if you're not already dead.

M Guilt does that.

A Because now I know that betrayal means nothing.

C Two women at the foot of a cross.

B A flower opens in the heat of the sun.

A A face screaming into hollow nothing.

B It's real, it's real, dead real, dead real.

M A private iconography which I cannot decipher,

A   Beyond my comprehension,

C   Beyond my

A   Beyond

B   There's a difference between articulacy and intelligence. I can't articulate the difference but there is one.

M   Empty.

A   Sickened.

C   White.

B   Love me.

A   Guilt lingers like the smell of death and nothing can free me from this cloud of blood.

C   You killed my mother.

A   She was already dead.

M   If you want me to abuse you I will abuse you.

A   She died.

B   People die.

M   It happens.

C   My entire life is waiting to see the person with whom I am currently obsessed, starving the weeks away until our next fifteen minute appointment.

A   MNO

C   I write the truth and it kills me.

B   On the run.

M   Nowhere to hide.

C   I hate these words that keep me alive
         I hate these words that won't let me die

B   Expressing my pain without easing it.

C   Ha ha ha

B Ho ho ho

M He he he

C It is not acceptable for me to be me.

A You're losing your mind in front of my eyes.

M It slipped silently out of control.

B Let me.

M Go.

A A small girl became increasingly paralysed by her parents' frequently violent rows. Sometimes she would spend hours standing completely still in the toilet, simply because that was where she happened to be when the fight began.
Finally, in moments of calm, she would take bottles of milk from the fridge or doorstep and leave them in places where she may later become trapped. Her parents were unable to understand why they found bottles of sour milk in every room in the house.

M Why?

C What?

B Why what?

C What?

M Why are you crying?

A There's no news here.

B You were so persistent.

C It's always me.

M You always knew this.

B It's out of control.

C How did I lose you?

A You threw me away.

C No.

M Yes.

B No.

A Yes.

B No.

C No.

A Yes.

　A beat.

B No.

C No.

M Yes.

B No.

C No.

A Yes.

C No.

　A beat.

A Yes.

C No.

B No.

M Yes.

A Yes.

M Yes.

C *(Emits a short one syllable scream.)*

　A beat.

C *(Emits a short one syllable scream.)*

B *(Emits a short one syllable scream.)*

M *(Emits a short one syllable scream.)*

B (*Emits a short one syllable scream.*)

A (*Emits a short one syllable scream.*)

M (*Emits a short one syllable scream.*)

C (*Emits a short one syllable scream.*)

   A beat.

M If you won't talk, I can't help you.

B This place.

C ES3.

A I am the beast at the end of the rope.

C Silence or violence.

B The choice is yours.

C Don't fill my stomach if you can't fill my heart.

B You fill my head as only someone who is absent can.

M Impaired judgement, sexual dysfunction, anxiety, headaches, nervousness, sleeplessness, restlessness, nausea, diarrhoea, itching, shaking, sweating, twitching.

C That's what I'm suffering from *now*.

M It's okay.

B It won't matter.

A It doesn't matter.

C Put me down or put me away.

A No one survives life.

C And no one can know what the night is like.

M Has it ever occurred to you you're in the wrong place?

C No.

B Never.

A No.

C If I die here I was murdered by daytime television.

A I lied for you and that is why I cannot love you.

M Do not demand,

A Do not entreat,

B Learn, learn, why can't I learn?

C They switch on my light every hour to check I'm still breathing.

B Again.

C I tell them sleep deprivation is a form of torture.

B Again and again.

M If you commit suicide you'll only have to come back go through it again.

B The same lesson, again and again.

A Thou shalt not kill thyself.

C Vanity, not sanity, will keep me intact.

M Do you ever hear voices?

B Only when they talk to me.

A Weary souls with dry mouths.

C I'm not ill, I just know that life is not worth living.

A I've lost my faith in honesty.

B Lost my faith in

M Forwards, upwards, onwards,

C Lost.

B 199714424

M Move on.

C I do not trust

M I do not care

C   Out, out into what?

A   A black fucking hole of half-love.

M   Move on.

A   I hate the consoled and the consoler.

C   I am much fucking angrier than you think.

A   I cannot trust you and I cannot respect you.

C   I am no longer honest.

A   You took that from me and I cannot love you.

M   Back to life.

C   An empty car park which I never can leave.

B   Fear rumbles over the city sky.

M   Absence sleeps between the buildings at night,

C   Between the cars in the lay-by,

B   Between the day and the night.

A   I have to be where I'm meant to be.

B   Let

C   Me

M   Go

A   The outside world is vastly overrated.

A pause.

C   Let the day perish in which I was born
Let the blackness of the night terrify it
Let the stars of its dawn be dark
May it not see the eyelids of the morning
Because it did not shut the door of my mother's womb

B   The thing that I fear comes upon me.

C   I hate you,

B   I need you,

M   Need more,

C   Need change.

A   All the totally predictable and sickening futility that is our relationship.

M   I want a real life,

B   A real love,

A   One that is rooted and grows upwards in daylight.

C   What's she got that I haven't got?

A   Me.

B   The things I want, I want with you.

M   It's just. Not. Me.

A   There are no secrets.

M   There is only blindness.

A   You've fallen in love with someone that doesn't exist.

C   No.

M   Yes.

B   No.

A   Yes.

C   No.

B   No.

M   Yes.

C   I knew this,

B   I knew this,

C   Why can't I learn?

A   I won't settle for a life in the dark.

B   Don't look at the sun, don't look at the sun.

C   I love you.

M Too late.

A It's over.

C (*Emits a formless cry of despair.*)

  A silence.

A We don't know we're born.

C What have they done to me? What have they done to me? What have they done to me? What have they done to me? What have they done to me? What have they done to me? What have they done to me? What have they done to me? What have they done to me? What have they done to me? What have they done to me? What have they done to me? What have they done to me? What have they done to me? What have they done to me? What have they done to me? What have they done to me?

M Grow up and stop blaming mother.

A Life happens.

B Like flowers,

C Like sunshine,

A Like nightfall.

C A motion away,

B Not a motion towards.

A It is not my fault.

C As if the direction makes any difference.

M Nobody knows.

B My heart is broken.

A It was never my fault.

M You kept coming back.

B Now and forever.

A I am not fighting for you any more.

B   The vision.

M   The loss.

C   The pain.

A   The loss.

B   The gain.

M   The loss.

C   The light.

B   If you died it would be like my bones had been removed. No one would know why, but I would collapse.

C   If I could be free of you,

B   If I could be free,

M   No that's not it,

A   No not at all,

B   That is not what I meant at all.

A   I broke her heart, what more do I want?

C   The vision.

M   The light.

C   The pain.

A   The light.

M   The gain.

B   The light.

C   The loss.

B   A circle is the only geometric shape defined by its centre. No chicken and egg about it, the centre came first, the circumference follows. The earth, by definition, has a centre. And only the fool that knows it can go wherever he pleases, knowing the centre will hold him down, stop him flying out of orbit. But when your sense of centre shifts, comes whizzing to the surface, the balance has gone. The balance has gone. The balance my baby has gone.

C When she left –

B The spine of my life is broken.

A Why is light given to one in misery

C Bring her back.

A And life to the bitter in soul

B If you were here –

M I am here.

A Like a deep summer shadow.

C I love her I miss her

B I'm through.

M Move on.

C Why did I not die at birth

M Come forth from the womb

B And expire

A Move in shadows, once in a fog.

M Pain is a shadow.

A The shadow of my lie.

C Red rock of ages

B You're not a bad person, you just think too much.

C Let me hide myself.

M Can you

C Would you

B Will you

M   Move on.

A   Never again I swear to Christ.

B   If I lose my voice I'm through.

M   Still here.

B   But I won't,

C   Not this time,

B   Not me.

C   Not yet.

M   It's like waiting for your hair to grow.

B   Estás astravesada como el día Miércoles.

C   That's me. Exist in the swing. Never still, never one thing or the other, always moving from one extreme to the furthest reaches of the other.

B   Sweet.

A   One touch.

B   So fucking sweet.

M   Record.

C   Where's my personality gone?

A   I'm too old for this.

M   Couldn't love you less.

B   Couldn't love you more.

M   To be perfectly honest,

C   (when am I ever 'perfectly honest'?)

B   Take no more.

   A beat.

C   This never happened.

   A silence.

A   What I sometimes mistake for ecstasy is simply the absence of grief.

M   Fear nothing.

B   All or nothing.

C   None of it,

B   All of it,

M   None.

C   I am an emotional plagiarist, stealing other people's pain, subsuming it into my own until

A   I can't remember

B   Whose

C   Any more

A   Maybe you're all right,

C   Maybe I'm bad,

A   But God has blessed me with the mark of Cain.

C   Weight.

B   Don't know.

M   Date.

A   Don't know.

B   Fate.

C   Don't know.

A   It's a punishment for hedging your bets.

M   Keep coming back.

B   Again and again.

A   The eternal return.

B   If I lose my voice I'm fucked.

C   Shit on a plate. Look enthusiastic or your own mother will take you apart.

M Get the Night Men in.

A My life is nothing special,

C A stream of haphazard events like any other,

A A stream into a salty ocean that stings, it stings, but does not kill.

M You're dead to me.

B An act of love.

C You're not my mother.

A We were many things.

B Something clicked.

M But I would never say that we were ever in love.

B Found her

A Loved her

C Lost her

M End.

A silence.

C Something has lifted,

A Outside the city,

B Before the shit started,

A Above the city,

C Another dream,

M I crossed a river that runs in shadow,

B In den Bergen, da fühlst du dich frei,

M One wish,

C A cool summer and a mild winter,

B No fights, no floods,

C   Darkness surrounds a collapsing star,

A   A long deep sleep with you in my arms,

B   No one nothing no shit,

C   Assimilated but not obliterated,

A   Peace,

M   A sickly glare with no single source,

A   A pale gold sea under a pale pink sky,

M   A distant bell crosses the empty sea,

B   Clouds converge as I see I am on a globe,

C   Waves sob like a pulse.

   A beat.

B   Here I am, once again, here I am, here I am, in the darkness, once again,

A   On the edge of nothing,

B   Here I am,

C   Hold my hand,

A   Glory be to the Father,

M   The truth is behind you,

B   I'd give it all up for you,

C   Into the light,

A   As it was in the beginning,

C   Beyond the darkness,

M   And ever shall be,

B   Into the light,

A   At the end of the day it comes back to this,

B   Gaining time,

A   It comes back to me,

M   But losing light,

A   It comes back to this,

C   Fat and shiny and dead dead dead serene,

M   I can't save you,

A   And clean.

C   Other lives

B   No fucker can.

M   Rolled into a ball.

A   Deliver my soul from the sword.

B   I wake as I dream,

M   Alone.

A   Which passeth all understanding.

C   I don't dream any more,

A   I have no dreams.

B   Gaining light,

C   I crossed a river,

M   But losing time.

B   I can't say no to you.

C   To be free of memory,

M   Free of desire,

C   Lie low, provoke nothing,

B   Say nothing.

A   Invisible.

C   When even dreams aren't private

B   Best to forget.

A   Random acts of meaningless joy.

M   You made love by the river.

All   Forget.

A beat.

B   Rape me.

A pause.

M   Is it possible?

C   Cured my body can't cure my soul.

A   I am so tired.

B   I keep coming back.

M   Be the one.

C   Patch and paint and paste a look onto my face.

B   My life in black and white in reverse.

M   Complete.

A   Do what thou wilt shall be the whole of the law.

M   Now.

A   Love is the law, love under will.

C   I feel nothing, nothing.
I feel nothing.

A   Satan, my lord, I am yours.

B   (*Quietly, continuously, until the end of* **A**'s *speech.*)
no no no no no no no/no no no no no no no no no

A   And don't forget that poetry is language for its own sake.
Don't forget when different words are sanctioned, other
attitudes required.
Don't forget decorum.
Don't forget decorum.

A beat.

B   Kill me.

A beat.

A   Free-falling

B   Into the light

C   Bright white light

A   World without end

C   You're dead to me

M   Glorious. Glorious.

B   And ever shall be

A   Happy

B   So happy

C   Happy and free.

Notes

Page 160 *El dinero viene solo.* (Spanish)
'Money comes alone.'

Page 167 *Meni ni iz džepa, ni u džep.* (Serbo-Croatian)
'It's neither in my pocket nor out of it.'

Page 172 *Du bist die Liebe meines Lebens.* (German)
'You are the love of my life.'

Page 176 *Besos brujos que me matan.* (Spanish)
'Witches' kisses that kill me.'

Page 179 *Jebem radoznale.* (Serbo-Croatian)
'I'm fucking the curious.'

Page 194 *Estás astravesada como el día Miércoles.* (Spanish)
'You are like a Wednesday.'

Page 196 *In den Bergen, da fühlst du dich frei.* (German)
'In the mountains, there you feel free.'

4.48 Psychosis

4.48 Psychosis was first performed at the Royal Court Jerwood Theatre Upstairs, London, on 23 June 2000. The cast was as follows:

Daniel Evans
Jo McInnes
Madeleine Potter

Directed by James Macdonald
Designed by Jeremy Herbert
Lighting by Nigel J Edwards
Sound by Paul Arditti

(A very long silence.)

– But you have friends.

(A long silence.)

You have a lot of friends.
What do you offer your friends to make them so
supportive?

(A long silence.)

What do you offer your friends to make them so
supportive?

(A long silence.)

What do you offer?

(Silence.)

– – – – –

a consolidated consciousness resides in a darkened banqueting
hall near the ceiling of a mind whose floor shifts as ten
thousand cockroaches when a shaft of light enters as all
thoughts unite in an instant of accord body no longer expellent
as the cockroaches comprise a truth which no one ever utters

I had a night in which everything was revealed to me.
How can I speak again?

the broken hermaphrodite who trusted hermself alone finds the
room in reality teeming and begs never to wake from the
nightmare

and they were all there
every last one of them
and they knew my name
as I scuttled like a beetle along the backs of their chairs

Remember the light and believe the light

An instant of clarity before eternal night

don't let me forget

– – – – –

I am sad

I feel that the future is hopeless and that things cannot improve

I am bored and dissatisfied with everything

I am a complete failure as a person

I am guilty, I am being punished

I would like to kill myself

I used to be able to cry but now I am beyond tears

I have lost interest in other people

I can't make decisions

I can't eat

I can't sleep

I can't think

I cannot overcome my loneliness, my fear, my disgust

I am fat

I cannot write

I cannot love

My brother is dying, my lover is dying, I am killing them both

I am charging towards my death

I am terrified of medication

I cannot make love

I cannot fuck

I cannot be alone

I cannot be with others

My hips are too big

I dislike my genitals

At 4.48
when desperation visits
I shall hang myself
to the sound of my lover's breathing

I do not want to die

I have become so depressed by the fact of my mortality that I
have decided to commit suicide

I do not want to live

I am jealous of my sleeping lover and covet his induced
unconsciousness

When he wakes he will envy my sleepless night of thought and
speech unslurred by medication

I have resigned myself to death this year

Some will call this self-indulgence
(they are lucky not to know its truth)
Some will know the simple fact of pain

This is becoming my normality

– – – – –

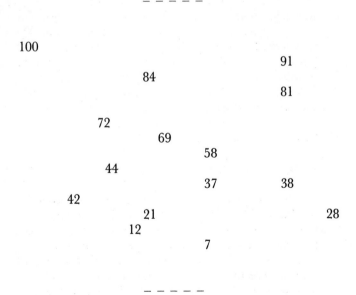

– – – – –

It wasn't for long, I wasn't there long. But drinking bitter black
coffee I catch that medicinal smell in a cloud of ancient

tobacco and something touches me in that still sobbing place and a wound from two years ago opens like a cadaver and a long buried shame roars its foul decaying grief.

A room of expressionless faces staring blankly at my pain, so devoid of meaning there must be evil intent.

Dr This and Dr That and Dr Whatsit who's just passing and thought he'd pop in to take the piss as well. Burning in a hot tunnel of dismay, my humiliation complete as I shake without reason and stumble over words and have nothing to say about my 'illness' which anyway amounts only to knowing that there's no point in anything because I'm going to die. And I am deadlocked by that smooth psychiatric voice of reason which tells me there is an objective reality in which my body and mind are one. But I am not here and never have been. Dr This writes it down and Dr That attempts a sympathetic murmur. Watching me, judging me, smelling the crippling failure oozing from my skin, my desperation clawing and all-consuming panic drenching me as I gape in horror at the world and wonder why everyone is smiling and looking at me with secret knowledge of my aching shame.

Shame shame shame.
Drown in your fucking shame.

Inscrutable doctors, sensible doctors, way-out doctors, doctors you'd think were fucking patients if you weren't shown proof otherwise, ask the same questions, put words in my mouth, offer chemical cures for congenital anguish and cover each other's arses until I want to scream for you, the only doctor who ever touched me voluntarily, who looked me in the eye, who laughed at my gallows humour spoken in the voice from the newly-dug grave, who took the piss when I shaved my head, who lied and said it was nice to see me. Who lied. And said it was nice to see me. I trusted you, I loved you, and it's not losing you that hurts me, but your bare-faced fucking falsehoods that masquerade as medical notes.

Your truth, your lies, not mine.

And while I was believing that you were different and that you maybe even felt the distress that sometimes flickered across your face and threatened to erupt, you were covering your arse too. Like every other stupid mortal cunt.

To my mind that's betrayal. And my mind is the subject of these bewildered fragments.

Nothing can extinguish my anger.

And nothing can restore my faith.

This is not a world in which I wish to live.

– – – – –

– Have you made any plans?

– Take an overdose, slash my wrists then hang myself.

– All those things together?

– It couldn't possibly be misconstrued as a cry for help.

(*Silence.*)

– It wouldn't work.

– Of course it would.

–   It wouldn't work. You'd start to feel sleepy from the overdose and wouldn't have the energy to cut your wrists.

(Silence.)

–   I'd be standing on a chair with a noose around my neck.

(Silence.)

–   If you were alone do you think you might harm yourself?

–   I'm scared I might.

–   Could that be protective?

–   Yes. It's fear that keeps me away from the train tracks. I just hope to God that death is the fucking end. I feel like I'm eighty years old. I'm tired of life and my mind wants to die.

–   That's a metaphor, not reality.

–   It's a simile.

–   That's not reality.

–   It's not a metaphor, it's a simile, but even if it were, the defining feature of a metaphor is that it's real.

(A long silence.)

–   You are not eighty years old.

(Silence.)

Are you?

(*A silence.*)

Are you?

(*A silence.*)

Or are you?

(*A long silence.*)

- Do you despise all unhappy people or is it me specifically?

- I don't despise you. It's not your fault. You're ill.

- I don't think so.

- No?

- No. I'm depressed. Depression is anger. It's what you did, who was there and who you're blaming.

- And who are you blaming?

- Myself.

– – – – –

Body and soul can never be married

I need to become who I already am and will bellow forever at this incongruity which has committed me to hell

Insoluble hoping cannot uphold me

I will drown in dysphoria
       in the cold black pond of my self
       the pit of my immaterial mind

How can I return to form
now my formal thought has gone?

Not a life that I could countenance.

They will love me for that which destroys me
       the sword in my dreams
       the dust of my thoughts
       the sickness that breeds in the folds of my mind

Every compliment takes a piece of my soul

An expressionist nag
Stalling between two fools
They know nothing –
       I have always walked free

Last in a long line of literary kleptomaniacs
       (a time honoured tradition)

Theft is the holy act
On a twisted path to expression

A glut of exclamation marks spells impending nervous
    breakdown
Just a word on a page and there is the drama

I write for the dead
    the unborn

After 4.48 I shall not speak again

I have reached the end of this dreary and repugnant
tale of a sense interned in an alien carcass and
lumpen by the malignant spirit of the moral majority

I have been dead for a long time

Back to my roots

                                     I sing without hope on the boundary

                     – – – – –

RSVP ASAP

                     – – – – –

Sometimes I turn around and catch the smell of you and I
cannot go on I cannot fucking go on without expressing
this terrible so fucking awful physical aching fucking longing
I have for you. And I cannot believe that I can feel this for
you and you feel nothing. Do you feel nothing?

(*Silence.*)

Do you feel nothing?

(*Silence.*)

And I go out at six in the morning and start my search for
you. If I've dreamt a message of a street or a pub or a
station I go there. And I wait for you.

(*Silence.*)

You know, I really feel like I'm being manipulated.

(*Silence.*)

I've never in my life had a problem giving another person what they want. But no one's ever been able to do that for me. No one touches me, no one gets near me. But now you've touched me somewhere so fucking deep I can't believe and I can't be that for you. Because I can't find you.

(*Silence.*)

What does she look like?
And how will I know her when I see her?
She'll die, she'll die, she'll only fucking die.

(*Silence.*)

Do you think it's possible for a person to be born in the wrong body?

(*Silence.*)

Do you think it's possible for a person to be born in the wrong era?

(*Silence.*)

Fuck you. Fuck you. Fuck you for rejecting me by never being there, fuck you for making me feel shit about myself, fuck you for bleeding the fucking love and life out of me, fuck my father for fucking up my life for good and fuck my mother for not leaving him, but most of all, fuck you God for making me love a person who does not exist,
FUCK YOU FUCK YOU FUCK YOU.

– – – – –

–   Oh dear, what's happened to your arm?

–   I cut it.

–   That's a very immature, attention seeking thing to do. Did it give you relief?

–   No.

–   Did it relieve the tension?

–   No.

–   Did it give you relief?

(*Silence.*)

Did it give you relief?

–   No.

–   I don't understand why you did that.

–   Then ask.

–   Did it relieve the tension?

(*A long silence.*)

Can I look?

–   No.

–   I'd like to look, to see if it's infected.

–   No.

(*Silence.*)

–   I thought you might do this. Lots of people do. It
     relieves the tension.

–   Have you ever done it?

–   . . .

–   No. Far too fucking sane and sensible. I don't know
     where you read that, but it does not relieve the
     tension.

     (*Silence.*)

     Why don't you ask me *why*?
     Why did I cut my arm?

–   Would you like to tell me?

–   Yes.

–   Then tell me.

–   ASK.
     ME.
     WHY.

     (*A long silence.*)

–   Why did you cut your arm?

–   Because it feels fucking great. Because it feels fucking
     amazing.

–   Can I look?

–   You can look. But don't touch.

–   (*Looks*) And you don't think you're ill?

–   No.

–   I do. It's not your fault. But you have to take
    responsibility for your own actions. Please don't do it
    again.

— – – – –

I dread the loss of her I've never touched
love keeps me a slave in a cage of tears
I gnaw my tongue with which to her I can never speak
I miss a woman who was never born
I kiss a woman across the years that say we shall never meet

> Everything passes
> Everything perishes
> Everything palls

> my thought walks away with a killing smile
> leaving discordant anxiety
> which roars in my soul

No hope No hope No hope No hope No hope No hope No hope

A song for my loved one, touching her absence
    the flux of her heart, the splash of her smile

In ten years time she'll still be dead. When I'm living with
it, dealing with it, when a few days pass when I don't even
think of it, she'll still be dead. When I'm an old lady living
on the street forgetting my name she'll still be dead, she'll
still be dead, it's just
                    fucking
                        over

                            and I must stand alone

My love, my love, why have you forsaken me?

She is the couching place where I never shall lie
and there's no meaning to life in the light of my loss

    Built to be lonely
    to love the absent

    Find me
    Free me
       from this

               corrosive doubt
               futile despair

               horror in repose

I can fill my space
fill my time
but nothing can fill this void in my heart

The vital need for which I would die

                          Breakdown

                – – – – –

–   No ifs or buts.

–   I didn't say if or but, I said no.

–   Can't must never have-to always won't should shan't.
    The unnegotiables.
    Not today.

    (*Silence.*)

–   Please. Don't switch off my mind by attempting to
    straighten me out. Listen and understand, and when
    you feel contempt don't express it, at least not
    verbally, at least not to me.

    (*Silence.*)

–   I don't feel contempt.

–   No?

–   No. It's not your fault.

–   It's not your fault, that's all I ever hear, it's not your
    fault, it's an illness, it's not your fault, I know it's not
    my fault. You've told me that so often I'm beginning
    to think it *is* my fault.

–   It's *not* your fault.

–   I KNOW.

–   But you allow it.

    (*Silence.*)

    Don't you?

–   There's not a drug on earth can make life meaningful.

–   You allow this state of desperate absurdity.

    (*Silence.*)

You allow it.

(*Silence.*)

– I won't be able to think. I won't be able to work.

– Nothing will interfere with your work like suicide.

(*Silence.*)

– I dreamt I went to the doctor's and she gave me eight minutes to live. I'd been sitting in the fucking waiting room half an hour.

(*A long silence.*)

Okay, let's do it, let's do the drugs, let's do the chemical lobotomy, let's shut down the higher functions of my brain and perhaps I'll be a bit more fucking capable of living.

Let's do it.

– – – – –

abstraction to the point of

unpleasant
unacceptable
uninspiring
impenetrable

irrelevant
irreverent
irreligious
unrepentant

dislike
dislocate
disembody
deconstruct

I don't imagine
     (clearly)
that a single soul
     could
          would
               should
                    or will

and if they did
I don't think
     (clearly)
that another soul
a soul like mine
     could
          would
               should
                    or will

irrespective

I know what I'm doing
     all too well

No native speaker

irrational
irreducible
irredeemable
unrecognisable

derailed
deranged
deform
free form

obscure to the point of

    True   Right   Correct
    Anyone or anybody
    Each   every   all

drowning in a sea of logic
                this monstrous state of palsy

          still ill

– – – – –

Symptoms: Not eating, not sleeping, not speaking, no sex
drive, in despair, wants to die.

Diagnosis: Pathological grief.

Sertraline, 50 mg. Insomnia worsened, severe anxiety,
anorexia, (weight loss 17kgs,) increase in suicidal thoughts,
plans and intention. Discontinued following hospitalization.

Zopiclone, 7.5mg. Slept. Discontinued following rash.
Patient attempted to leave hospital against medical advice.
Restrained by three male nurses twice her size. Patient

threatening and uncooperative. Paranoid thoughts –
believes hospital staff are attempting to poison her.

Melleril, 50mg. Co-operative.

Lofepramine, 70mg, increased to 140mg, then 210mg.
Weight gain 12kgs. Short term memory loss. No other
reaction.

Argument with junior doctor whom she accused of
treachery after which she shaved her head and cut her
arms with a razor blade.

Patient discharged into the care of the community on
arrival of acutely psychotic patient in emergency clinic in
greater need of a hospital bed.

Citalopram, 20mg. Morning tremors. No other reaction.

Lofepramine and Citalopram discontinued after patient got
pissed off with side affects and lack of obvious improvement.
Discontinuation symptoms: Dizziness and confusion. Patient
kept falling over, fainting and walking out in front of cars.
Delusional ideas – believes consultant is the antichrist.

Fluoxetine hydrochloride, trade name Prozac, 20mg,
increased to 40mg. Insomnia, erratic appetite, (weight loss
14kgs,) severe anxiety, unable to reach orgasm, homicidal
thoughts towards several doctors and drug manufacturers.
Discontinued.

Mood: Fucking angry.
Affect: Very angry.

Thorazine, 100mg. Slept. Calmer.

Venlafaxine, 75mg, increased to 150mg, then 225mg.
Dizziness, low blood pressure, headaches. No other
reaction. Discontinued.

Patient declined Seroxat. Hypochondria – cites spasmodic
blinking and severe memory loss as evidence of tardive
dyskinesia and tardive dementia.

Refused all further treatment.

100 aspirin and one bottle of Bulgarian Cabernet
Sauvignon, 1986. Patient woke in a pool of vomit and said
'Sleep with a dog and rise full of fleas.' Severe stomach
pain. No other reaction.

– – – – –

Hatch opens
Stark light

          the television talks
          full of eyes
          the spirits of sight

                    and now I am so afraid

          I'm seeing things
          I'm hearing things
          I don't know who I am

               tongue out
                         thought stalled

          the piecemeal crumple of my mind

Where do I start?
Where do I stop?
How do I start?
(As I mean to go on)

How do I stop?
How do I stop?
How do I stop?
How do I stop?
How do I stop?   A tab of pain
How do I stop?   Stabbing my lungs
How do I stop?   A tab of death
How do I stop?   Squeezing my heart

        I'll die
                not yet
                        but it's there

Please . . .
Money . . .
Wife . . .

Every act is a symbol
the weight of which crushes me

A dotted line on the throat
            CUT HERE

DON'T LET THIS KILL ME
THIS WILL KILL ME AND CRUSH ME AND
    SEND ME TO HELL

I beg you to save me from this madness that eats me
        a sub-intentional death

I thought I should never speak again
but now I know there is something blacker than desire

perhaps it will save me
perhaps it will kill me

a dismal whistle that is the cry of heartbreak around the
hellish bowl at the ceiling of my mind

a blanket of roaches

cease this war

My legs are empty
Nothing to say
And this is the rhythm of madness

_ _ _ _ _

–   I gassed the Jews, I killed the Kurds, I bombed the
    Arabs, I fucked small children while they begged for
    mercy, the killing fields are mine, everyone left the
    party because of me, I'll suck your fucking eyes out
    send them to your mother in a box and when I die
    I'm going to be reincarnated as your child only fifty
    times worse and as mad as all fuck I'm going to make
    your life a living fucking hell I REFUSE I REFUSE I
    REFUSE LOOK AWAY FROM ME

–   It's all right.

–   LOOK AWAY FROM ME

—   It's all right. I'm here.

—   Look away from me

        – – – – –

We are anathema
the pariahs of reason

Why am I stricken?
       I saw visions of God

and it shall come to pass

Gird yourselves:
for ye shall be broken in pieces
it shall come to pass

Behold the light of despair
the glare of anguish
and ye shall be driven to darkness

If there is blasting
       (there shall be blasting)
the names of offenders shall be shouted from the rooftops

Fear God
       and his wicked convocation

a scall on my skin, a seethe in my heart
a blanket of roaches on which we dance
this infernal state of siege

All this shall come to pass
all the words of my noisome breath

Remember the light and believe the light

Christ is dead
            and the monks are in ecstasy

We are the abjects
who depose our leaders
and burn incense unto Baal

Come now, let us reason together
Sanity is found in the mountain of the Lord's house on the
   horizon of the soul that eternally recedes
The head is sick, the heart's caul torn
Tread the ground on which wisdom walks
Embrace beautiful lies –
   the chronic insanity of the sane

                        the wrenching begins

                    – – – – –

–   At 4.48
    when sanity visits
    for one hour and twelve minutes I am in my right mind.
    When it has passed I shall be gone again,
    a fragmented puppet, a grotesque fool.
    Now I am here I can see myself
    but when I am charmed by vile delusions of happiness,
    the foul magic of this engine of sorcery,
    I cannot touch my essential self.

    Why do you believe me then and not now?

    Remember the light and believe the light.
    Nothing matters more.
    Stop judging by appearances and make a right judgement.

−   It's all right. You will get better.

−   Your disbelief cures nothing.

    Look away from me.

              − − − − −

Hatch opens
Stark light

A table two chairs and no windows

Here am I
and there is my body

                    dancing on glass

In accident time where there are no accidents

              You have no choice
              the choice comes after

Cut out my tongue
tear out my hair
cut off my limbs
but leave me my love
I would rather have lost my legs
pulled out my teeth
gouged out my eyes
than lost my love

flash flicker slash burn wring press dab slash
flash flicker punch burn float flicker dab flicker
punch flicker flash burn dab press wring press
punch flicker float burn flash flicker burn

it will never pass

dab flicker punch slash wring slash punch slash
float flicker flash punch wring press flash press
dab flicker wring burn flicker dab flash dab float
burn press burn flicker burn flash

Nothing's forever

(but Nothing)

slash wring punch burn flicker dab float dab
flicker burn punch burn flash dab press dab
wring flicker float slash burn slash punch slash
press slash float slash flicker burn dab

Victim. Perpetrator. Bystander.

punch burn float flicker flash flicker burn slash
wring press dab slash flash flicker dab flicker
punch flicker flash burn dab press flicker wring
press punch flash flicker burn flicker flash

the morning brings defeat

wring slash punch slash float flicker flash punch
wring dab flicker punch slash press flash press
dab flicker wring burn flicker dab flash dab float
burn press burn flash flicker slash

>   beautiful pain
>   that says I exist

flicker punch slash dab wring press burn slash
press slash punch flicker flash press burn slash
dab flicker float flash flicker dab press burn slash
press slash punch flash flicker burn

>   and a saner life tomorrow

– – – – –

100
93
86
79
72
65
58
51
44
37
30
23
16
9
2

– – – – –

Sanity is found at the centre of convulsion, where madness is scorched from the bisected soul.

I know myself.

I see myself.

My life is caught in a web of reason
    spun by a doctor to augment the sane.

At 4.48

                I shall sleep.

I came to you hoping to be healed.

You are my doctor, my saviour, my omnipotent judge, my priest, my god, the surgeon of my soul.

And I am your proselyte to sanity.

        – – – – –

to achieve goals and ambitions

to overcome obstacles and attain a high standard

to increase self-regard by the successful exercise of talent

to overcome opposition

to have control and influence over others

to defend myself

to defend my psychological space

to vindicate the ego

to receive attention

to be seen and heard

to excite, amaze, fascinate, shock, intrigue, amuse, entertain
or entice others

to be free from social restrictions

to resist coercion and constriction

to be independent and act according to desire

to defy convention

to avoid pain

to avoid shame

to obliterate past humiliation by resumed action

to maintain self-respect

to repress fear

to overcome weakness

to belong

to be accepted

to draw close and enjoyably reciprocate with another

to converse in a friendly manner, to tell stories, exchange
sentiments, ideas, secrets

to communicate, to converse

to laugh and make jokes

to win affection of desired Other

to adhere and remain loyal to Other

to enjoy sensuous experiences with cathected Other

to feed, help, protect, comfort, console, support, nurse or
heal

to be fed, helped, protected, comforted, consoled,
supported, nursed or healed

to form mutually enjoyable, enduring, cooperating and
reciprocating relationship with Other, with an equal

to be forgiven

to be loved

to be free

– – – – –

– You've seen the worst of me.

– Yes.

– I know nothing of you.

– No.

– But I like you.

– I like you.

  (*Silence.*)

– You're my last hope.

  (*A long silence.*)

– You don't need a friend you need a doctor.

  (*A long silence.*)

– You are so wrong.

  (*A very long silence.*)

– But you have friends.

  (*A long silence.*)

  You have a lot of friends.
  What do you offer your friends to make them so
  supportive?

  (*A long silence.*)

  What do you offer your friends to make them so
  supportive?

  (*A long silence.*)

What do you offer?

(*Silence.*)

We have a professional relationship. I think we have a
good relationship. But it's professional.

(*Silence.*)

I feel your pain but I cannot hold your life in my
hands.

(*Silence.*)

You'll be all right. You're strong. I know you'll be
okay because I like you and you can't like someone
who doesn't like themself. The people I fear for are
the ones I don't like because they hate themselves so
much they won't let anyone else like them either. But
I do like you. I'll miss you. And I know you'll be ok.

(*Silence.*)

Most of my clients want to kill me. When I walk out
of here at the end of the day I need to go home to
my lover and relax. I need to be with my friends and
relax. I need my friends to be really together.

(*Silence.*)

I fucking hate this job and I need my friends to be
sane.

(*Silence.*)

I'm sorry.

—   It's not my fault.

—   I'm sorry, that was a mistake.

—   It is not my fault.

—   No. It's not your fault. I'm sorry.

(*Silence.*)

I was trying to explain —

—   I know. I'm angry because I understand, not because I
     don't.

                    — — — — —

Fattened up
  Shored up
    Shoved out

my body decompensates
my body flies apart

no way to reach out
beyond the reaching out I've already done

you will always have a piece of me
because you held my life in your hands

those brutal hands

this will end me

I thought it was silent
till it went silent

how have you inspired this pain?

I've never understood
what it is I'm not supposed to feel
like a bird on the wing in a swollen sky
my mind is torn by lightning
as it flies from the thunder behind

Hatch opens
Stark light
and Nothing
Nothing
see Nothing

What am I like?
                    the child of negation

out of one torture chamber into another
a vile succession of errors without remission
every step of the way I've fallen

Despair propels me to suicide
Anguish for which doctors can find no cure
Nor care to understand
I hope you never understand
Because I like you

I like you
I like you

still black water
as deep as forever
as cold as the sky
as still as my heart when your voice is gone
I shall freeze in hell

of course I love you
you saved my life

I wish you hadn't
I wish you hadn't
I wish you'd left me alone

a black and white film of yes or no yes or no yes or no yes
or no yes or no yes or no

I've always loved you
                    even when I hated you

What am I like?
                    just like my father

oh no oh no oh no

Hatch opens
Stark light

                                        the rupture begins

I don't know where to look any more

Tired of crowd searching
  Telepathy
    and hope

Watch the stars
predict the past
    and change the world with a silver eclipse

the only thing that's permanent is destruction
we're all going to disappear
trying to leave a mark more permanent than myself

I've not killed myself before so don't look for precedents
What came before was just the beginning

    a cyclical fear
    that's not the moon it's the earth
    A revolution

       Dear God, dear God, what shall I do?

    All I know
    is snow
           and black despair

    Nowhere left to turn
      an ineffectual moral spasm
      the only alternative to murder

Please don't cut me up to find out how I died
I'll tell you how I died

One hundred Lofepramine, forty five Zopiclone, twenty five
Temazepam, and twenty Melleril

Everything I had

Swallowed

Slit

Hung

It is done

    behold the Eunuch
      of castrated thought

    skull
    unwound

    the capture
     the rapture
      the rupture
       of a soul

    a solo symphony

    at 4.48
    the happy hour
    when clarity visits

    warm darkness
    which soaks my eyes

    I know no sin

    this is the sickness of becoming great

    this vital need for which I would die

to be loved

I'm dying for one who doesn't care
I'm dying for one who doesn't know

you're breaking me

Speak
Speak
Speak

ten yard ring of failure
look away from me

My final stand

No one speaks

Validate me
Witness me
See me
Love me

my final submission
my final defeat

the chicken's still dancing
the chicken won't stop

I think that you think of me
the way I'd have you think of me

the final period
the final full stop

look after your mum now
look after your mum

Black snow falls

in death you hold me

never free

I have no desire for death
no suicide ever had

watch me vanish
watch me

vanish

watch me

watch me

watch

It is myself I have never met, whose face is pasted on the underside of my mind

please open the curtains

_ _ _ _ _

Skin

a ten minute film

Skin was first transmitted on Channel 4 on 17 June 1997.
The cast was as follows:

Billy	Ewen Bremner
Marcia	Marcia Rose
Kath	Agnieszke Liggett
Neville	Yemi Ajibade
Mother	Dave Atkins
Terry	James Bannon
Martin	Dominic Brunt
Nick	Gregory Donaldson

Director Vincent O'Connell
Director of photography Seamus McGarvey
Editor Victoria Boydell
Producer Nick Love
Executive producers Polly Tapson and Charles Steele
Production finance British Screen/Channel 4

Characters

Billy
Marcia
Kath
Neville
Mother
Terry
Martin
Nick

1. INT. DAY. BILLY'S FLAT.

BILLY is asleep, a lump under a floral duvet. Sunlight is streaming in through the window of his messy South London bedsit. The telephone rings and the answerphone clicks on.

> ANSWERPHONE (BILLY)
>
> Hello, I'm asleep, leave a message,
> call you back, cheers.

As we listen to the message, we pan around the room. There is a cuddly polar bear at the foot of the bed. A photo of a smiling middle-aged woman. A baseball bat. Rubbish lined up in size order around the skirting board, and in the middle of the room, a model castle made from empty cigarette packets and boxes of mushroom flavoured cup-a-soup. The phone beeps and the lump under the covers groans and begins to move.

> ANSWERPHONE (TERRY)
>
> Billyboy, it's me. You awake? Pick up the
> phone you idle sod.

BILLY's hand emerges from under the covers, giving the phone the finger.

> ANSWERPHONE (TERRY)
>
> Suit yourself. See you at three. Smash the bastards.

He hangs up and the answerphone resets itself. BILLY's head emerges from under the cover. He is a skinhead. He gets out of bed and stands naked in front of the window. He is painfully thin. On his back is a large skull. On his right arm is a Union Jack, on his left a bulldog, on one of his forearms a series of blue dots, and over his heart 'Mum'. He presses the play button on the answerphone and listens to the message again.

ANSWERPHONE (TERRY)

Billyboy, it's me. You awake? Pick up the
phone you idle sod. (PAUSE) Suit yourself.
See you at three. Smash the bastards.

As he listens, BILLY looks out of the window. NEVILLE,
an old black man who also has a bedsit in the house, is
tending a large plot of thriving cannabis plants which have
taken over the garden. There is a large colourful
homemade shed for his tools with a deckchair outside it.
BILLY and NEVILLE make eye-contact. NEVILLE gives a
half-nod of recognition. BILLY points at him. NEVILLE
shakes his head and goes back to his plants.

BILLY looks up at the house opposite. He sees a black
woman staring at him from one of the windows. BILLY
grabs his penis and makes wanking gestures at her. She
stares and then laughs. BILLY laughs too. She goes away,
smiling, leaving BILLY staring sadly at her window. BILLY
goes to the sink and looks at his face in the mirror. He
smiles. Then grimaces. He tries to look hard, then gives up,
giggling. He runs a hand over his bristly head. The phone
rings. Fast cutting as we listen to the message – BILLY
shaving his head and chin, tipping shampoo onto his almost
bald head, rinsing his head under the tap, scrubbing his
neck, applying conditioner, cleaning his teeth, spraying
deodorant under his arms, patting aftershave onto his face
and neck and kissing his reflection.

ANSWERPHONE (BILLY)

Hello, I'm asleep, leave a message,
call you back, cheers.

ANSWERPHONE (MOTHER)

William, it's me. Mum. I'm very
worried about you.

BILLY draws a black swastika on his right fist.

cut to/

2. INT. DAY. A CAFE IN SOUTH LONDON.

MOTHER, the cafe owner, a big man with a fag in his
mouth, is serving breakfasts to a group of skins who have
taken over a large table in the centre of the cafe. They all
eat, except BILLY, who is chain-smoking.

MOTHER

Two English extra rasher, two English extra sausage,
one double English, one banana and ketchup omelette,
two English extra toast.

TERRY

Thank you, Mother. Sausage, Bill?

BILLY looks disgusted and they all laugh at him. TERRY
splats some ketchup on his food as he talks, and puts the
bottle in his pocket. MARTIN sprinkles pepper on his food,
and pockets the pepperpot.

TERRY

Wanna get yourself sorted, Billyboy.

BILLY

I'm all right.

TERRY

Not just your head, get some meat on your bones.

MARTIN

Your bone in some meat.

NICK

Your meat in her mouth.

TERRY

Your mouth round some meat.

TERRY presents BILLY with a sausage that he doesn't take.

BILLY

I'm all right.

TERRY

I do hope you're not turning
into a vegetarian, Billy.

A phone rings. All of the skins except BILLY pull out a mobile and shout 'Yeah' into it, repeatedly and with increasing annoyance, even when one of them, NICK, has got an answer.

NICK (INTO PHONE)

Where are you, Vincent? We expected
you at three.

BILLY notices an eight-year-old mixed-race BOY outside the cafe. He is holding a cuddly polar bear and staring in at the group, his face pressed up against the glass. He is smiling.

MARTIN

You're not looking good, Bill.

TERRY

He don't fucking eat.

MARTIN

Look a bit tense.

TERRY

Can't do nothing if you're a skinny little fuckwit.

NICK

May as well be something else.

MARTIN

Or nothing at all.

BILLY

FUCK OFF.

The others stop talking and barking down their mobiles, and look at him, then at the BOY. BILLY holds up his fist, showing the BOY his swastika. The BOY bursts out laughing. BILLY gets up, furious. The BOY runs off, laughing. BILLY sits and TERRY pushes a plate of food over to him.

TERRY

Get it down you, Bill.

BILLY

It's a pig's arse, Tel.

TERRY and BILLY stare at each other. BILLY touches his cigarette end to a sausage skin, burning through it, then squeezes the meat out.

BILLY

Brain and bollock, innard and eyelid,
toenail and teeth, all wrapped up in a
pig's foreskin.

He drops the empty sausage skin in disgust. MARTIN spits out a mouthful of sausage and looks at it closely. He puts his fork down. Everyone stops eating.

> MOTHER
>
> Good grub, that.

> MARTIN
>
> Sorry, Mother.

BILLY grinds his cigarette into the meat and gets up to leave. He takes a banana from the counter, dumping some change down in its place. The others follow, tossing coins at MOTHER, and BILLY pretends to shoot them with the banana.

> MOTHER (TO BILLY)
>
> Oi! They're not for eating.

cut to/

3. EXT. DAY. A CHURCH IN BRIXTON.

BILLY and the gang arrive outside the church as the black bride and white groom emerge to the sound of bells. They are showered with confetti and smile happily as the white PHOTOGRAPHER begins to manoeuvre the two families into one. A black TEENAGER wanders around with a camcorder making a more informal record of the event. The skins are noticed by a group of young black men in suits, the bride's brothers and friends, who innocuously put themselves between the skins and the couple. Led by TERRY, the skins walk up close to the black men.

BILLY puts his hand inside his jacket and draws the

banana. He peels it slowly and eats it. He throws the skin
at one of the men, who smiles contemptuously and wipes
the mess off his suit. The distinctive sound of monkey
noises begins from BILLY. MARTIN joins in and the
sound grows. The black men's faces, impassive, bored, then
disgusted, intercut with the ridiculously contorted faces of
the skins doing ape impressions. One of the youngest black
men takes a step towards the skins. TERRY pulls out the
sauce bottle stolen from the cafe and smashes it into his
face, ketchup flying everywhere. The smallest of beats, then
everyone attacks.

We see boots in faces, knees in groins, headbutts making
contact, a fork being stabbed into someone's leg, pepper
thrown into someone's eyes; as well as women seizing their
children and being ushered back into the church by
husbands and fathers. The PHOTOGRAPHER hesitates,
then turns his camera on the fight and clicks the shutter
rapidly. MARTIN notices, snatches the camera and
smashes it in the PHOTOGRAPHER's face, breaking his
nose. MARTIN takes a picture of him, then drops the
camera on his sprawling body. The camcorder
TEENAGER is caught in the middle of the fight, his
camera whizzing around as he tries to get out.

BILLY is holding his own – he's hurt but has done enough
to have exhilaration all over his face. He gets hit hard on
the back of the head and goes down heavily. We see him
kiss his swastika hand, then reach out and find a brick. He
stands up and smashes the brick down onto the nearest
black head. Over and over, as hard as he can, hatred and
revulsion all over his face, blood pouring from his head.
TERRY is pulling him away, shouting over the bells.

TERRY

Pigs.

BILLY drops the brick and runs as police swarm
everywhere, arresting motionless bodies on the ground and

kicking both blacks and skins when they can. BILLY dashes
down an alleyway and slumps against the wall. Police run
past and it is silent. BILLY gives a shout of triumph.

cut to/

4. INT. DAY. THE BATHROOM.

BILLY is in the shower. He winces when water runs
directly onto his head wound. He rubs soap vigorously into
every bit of himself except his right hand where the
swastika is. There is a knock on the bathroom door. BILLY
rinses the soap off, gets out of the shower and dries himself.
He sits on the toilet and has a crap. He wraps a towel
around his waist and opens the bathroom door. NEVILLE
is outside. He nods at BILLY and goes into the bathroom.
He looks down the toilet, then at BILLY, who is grinning.
He shakes his head.

NEVILLE

Silly boy.

He pulls the chain and closes the bathroom door.

cut to/

5. INT. DAY. BILLY'S FLAT.

BILLY is looking in the mirror, trying to look at the back
of his head as he listens to his answerphone messages. He
dresses in tight blue jeans, white tee-shirt, red braces and
cherry red docs.

ANSWERPHONE (TERRY)

Billyboy, you all right? We lost you.
You pulped that bloke. Nice one, mate.

ANSWERPHONE (MARTIN)

'S Martin. How's your head? You got
our tickets. 7.30. Don't forget.

The black woman appears at the window opposite. BILLY
smiles tentatively. She looks back, then beckons him. They
stare at each other and she disappears. BILLY looks at
himself in the mirror.

cut to/

6. INT. DAY. THE HALLWAY.

BILLY runs down the stairs – he is now wearing a pair of
black baggy jeans, tee-shirt and a black denim jacket.

cut to/

7. EXT. DAY. THE STREET.

BILLY crosses the road to the house opposite, passing
NEVILLE, apparently asleep in his deckchair. When
BILLY has passed, NEVILLE opens one eye, then both
when he sees BILLY's clothes. He thinks about it for a
moment, then loses interest and settles down to sleep again.
BILLY stands at the door of the house opposite and looks
for a doorbell. He can't find one, so knocks on the door
with his bare knuckles. A young white woman answers the
door, KATH. She has a shaven head, wears tight blue
jeans, white tee-shirt, red braces and cherry red docs. Her
dog stands next to her. KATH and BILLY look at each
other surprised.

BILLY

I'm . . . there's a woman lives here. Second floor.
Black. Don't know her name.

KATH

Marcia.

BILLY

Yeah, Marcia. She in?

KATH

No.

MARCIA appears at the bottom of the stairs.

BILLY

Hello.

She smiles. BILLY pats the dog.

cut to/

8. INT. DAY. MARCIA'S FLAT.

BILLY is standing nervously in MARCIA's bedroom looking at a pyramid of tin cans. MARCIA is sitting on the bed. BILLY reaches out to take a can off the pyramid.

MARCIA

Can sit down if you like.

BILLY looks out of the window back at his own bedsit.

BILLY

Looks different from here.

MARCIA

What happened to your head?

BILLY

Went on a march.

MARCIA looks closely at his wound, then gets a bottle and some cotton wool from a cabinet. She dabs his head carefully.

MARCIA

Witch-hazel.

BILLY takes her hand and examines it. He smiles. She touches his swastika.

BILLY

'S funny.

MARCIA

What?

BILLY

Soft skin.

MARCIA

You never touched a black woman before?

BILLY

Only with a baseball bat.

They stare at each other. MARCIA moves down onto the floor, still holding BILLY's swastika hand. She lies on her front and props herself up on her elbow, pulling BILLY down too, their hands linked in front of them, eyes locked. They begin to arm wrestle. Their faces are close, looking into each other's eyes. It's a close battle. BILLY screams in humiliation as she wins. MARCIA smiles. He stares at her.

BILLY

Can I kiss you?

She takes his face in her hands and kisses him. They kiss deeply.

MARCIA

I'm black.

He kisses her more passionately. She takes off his jacket. He takes off her top then his own tee-shirt. They lie on the floor kissing, running their hands over each other's skin with wonder. They become frantic. MARCIA tears off the rest of her clothes and BILLY's trousers. He is wearing Union Jack boxer shorts. MARCIA stops, and then laughs. BILLY looks sheepish and slips off the shorts. They lie on the bed together, kissing tenderly. The kissing becomes more passionate. MARCIA holds BILLY down, climbs on top of him, and fucks him. He comes quickly.

BILLY

Sorry.

MARCIA picks up the boxer shorts and examines them. She rips them up. An idea occurs to her, and she takes BILLY's hands gently and ties them to the bedstead with the shorts. BILLY laughs nervously. She frowns at him.

MARCIA

Again.

They wait, then BILLY begins to move slowly again, concentrating hard. He moves faster and faster until he's fucking her hard. She comes with a shout.

cut to/

9. INT. DAY. MARCIA'S FLAT.

Later. BILLY is blindfolded, hands tied behind his back.
He is licking, kissing and smelling MARCIA's skin as she
presents different parts of her body to his face. She has a
hand stuffed in her mouth to stop her making any noise.
She's terrified.

cut to/

10. INT. NIGHT. MARCIA'S FLAT.

MARCIA is fucking semi-conscious BILLY, slapping him
around the head and face hard.

MARCIA

What's it like? What's it like? What's it like?
What's it like? What's it like? What's it like?

BILLY covers his head to defend himself from the blows
and doesn't answer. MARCIA continues to batter him.

cut to/

11. INT. NIGHT. MARCIA'S FLAT.

MARCIA is staring at the pyramid of tins as if she has
never seen it before. She reaches out slowly and takes a
can from the top. She puts a bowl down in front of
BILLY's face. He is crouching on the floor, naked.
MARCIA opens the tin, then strokes his bare back.

MARCIA

Nothing of you.

She tips the contents of the tin into the bowl. It is dog
food. BILLY sniffs it, and looks up at her through
blackened eyes, disgusted.

MARCIA

You bruise easy.

cut to/

12. INT. EARLY MORNING. MARCIA'S FLAT.

BILLY is on his back on the bed, tied up. MARCIA is sitting astride him with a razor. She shaves his chest, legs, eyebrows and pubic hair. BILLY lies very still.

cut to/

13. INT. MORNING. MARCIA'S FLAT.

MARCIA is scrubbing BILLY's tattoos with a stiff brush and bleach. The skin is raw and bleeding, and BILLY is screaming in pain. MARCIA removes the swastika, then kisses his hand.

cut to/

14. INT. DAY. MARCIA'S FLAT.

BILLY is tied to the bed, lying on his front, spread-eagled. MARCIA is cutting her name into his back with a stanley knife. She cries silently, and licks away the blood.

cut to/

15. INT. NIGHT. MARCIA'S FLAT.

MARCIA is sitting on the table, curled up, very still and silent. BILLY is crawling around the floor, reaching for her.

> BILLY
>
> Please. Please. Where are you?
> Please. Marcia. Please.

She closes her eyes and doesn't make a sound.

cut to/

16. INT. MORNING. MARCIA'S FLAT.

MARCIA is asleep. BILLY looks at her closely. He picks up her clothes and slowly puts them on, layer by layer, until he's dressed as a woman. He sits at her feet and hugs the clothes to him.

> BILLY
>
> Mum.

cut to/

17. INT. DAY. MARCIA'S FLAT.

MARCIA is lying in bed watching BILLY dress painfully. When he's fully dressed he sits on the edge of the bed and stares at her.

> BILLY
>
> I really like you.

> MARCIA
>
> No you don't.

BILLY looks at the floor. The dog bowl is empty.

BILLY
Do you know him?

MARCIA
Who?

BILLY
That bloke at the wedding got his head smashed in.

MARCIA
Not personally.

BILLY
Why don't you like me?

MARCIA
Why don't you like me?

BILLY
Can I stay?

MARCIA
(THINKS.) I don't think so.

BILLY
I'd like to.

MARCIA
It's not a good idea.

BILLY
Please.

MARCIA
It wouldn't work.

BILLY

I'd –

MARCIA

Don't want you, Billy.

BILLY

I did what you said.

MARCIA

Don't want you.

BILLY thinks about it, then gets up and leaves.

cut to/

18. EXT. DAY. THE STREET.

BILLY strides across the road, tight with anger. He stops by a car and kicks the lights in. NEVILLE is painting a large smiley face on the side of his shed. He turns and watches BILLY kick the car, then looks up to MARCIA's window. BILLY goes into the house. NEVILLE turns the smiley face into a sad one, and paints on tears.

cut to/

19. INT. DAY. THE HALLWAY.

BILLY thunders up the stairs.

cut to/

20. INT. DAY. BILLY'S FLAT.

BILLY slams the door and tears off his clothes. He looks at his face in the mirror. It is cut and bruised, he has no eyebrows and his tattoos are bleeding.

> BILLY
>
> You cunt.

He starts to cry. He punches the mirror, breaking it. He opens the cabinet and takes out a bottle of painkillers. He takes two. He looks at his splintered face in the mirror.

> BILLY
>
> No more Billy.

He tips a handful of pills into his palm. He puts them in his mouth. He gets a can of beer from the fridge and goes to the window, naked. He looks at MARCIA's window. She isn't there. He swigs some beer and swallows the pills. He drinks the rest of the can quickly. He waits for something to happen. Nothing. He leaves a new message on the answerphone.

> BILLY
>
> Hello. I'm dead. Don't bother
> to leave a message.

He lights a cigarette and waits. He looks down to the garden and sees NEVILLE looking up at him.

cut to/

21. EXT. DAY. THE STREET.

NEVILLE's POV, looking up at BILLY. BILLY smiles, then falls backwards out of view.

cut to/

22. INT. DAY. MARCIA'S ROOM.

MARCIA is lying in bed, her face to the wall. She is crying. KATH comes in. She watches MARCIA's back for a moment. MARCIA doesn't move. KATH gets into bed with MARCIA, fully clothed, and wraps her arms around her from behind. A silence.

MARCIA

I'm sorry.

A silence.

KATH

It doesn't matter.

MARCIA turns around and buries her face in KATH's chest.

cut to/

23. INT. DAY. THE HALLWAY.

NEVILLE is dragging BILLY along by the ankles. BILLY is naked and unconscious. His head bangs on the door frame and bumps down steps.

cut to/

24. INT. DAY. THE BATHROOM.

BILLY is vomiting violently down the toilet. NEVILLE kneels beside him, patting his back.

NEVILLE

You're all right, white boy, you're all right.

BILLY vomits some more.

NEVILLE

That's it son, better out than in, you're all right.

BILLY looks into the old man's face and smiles weakly. He begins to sob. Then rests his head on the toilet seat and cries his heart out. Freeze frame on his face. Picture bleaches, then whites out.

– e n d –

For a complete catalogue of Methuen Drama titles
write to:

Methuen Drama
A & C Black Publishers Limited
38 Soho Square
London
W1D 3HB

or you can visit our website at:

www.acblack.com